·Choos

Cope

·Mary J. Beggs·

RadiantBOOKS ♨ 》》

Gospel Publishing House
Springfield, Missouri
02–0510

Library of Congress Catalog Card Number 87–82988
International Standard Book Number 0–88243–510–8
Printed in the United States of America

What I did or was yesterday, or in yesteryears,
I perhaps can't help or change. But today . . .
I have a choice.

Mary J. Beggs

Table of Contents

Foreword   7
Preface   9
Acknowledgments   10
Introduction   11

PART ONE
  1. The Promise   17
  2. Just Like Mama   28
  3. The Hiding Game   36
  4. Substitute Mother   42
  5. Together We Can   56
  6. Grief Without Tears   65

PART TWO
  7. The Year of the Curse   75
  8. Looking for Answers   84
  9. Hold Me   90

10. Taking Off the Smiles   97

11. Ministry Vs. Marriage?   105

12. Learning To Lean   110

13. Weapons for the Fight   118

Epilogue   124

Foreword

There is a tendency for children who grow up around illness to develop the symptoms of that illness—but only the symptoms. However, unless coping mechanisms are deliberately changed by such children, the symptoms can be exaggerated in each succeeding generation.

Mrs. Beggs is to be congratulated for bearing her soul for others to witness her heartache and pain. A weaker soul would have tried to hide behind the symptoms and slip into an ineffective life-style or tried to keep up a false front, pretending that all was well. But, by choice, she has exposed the trauma as she perceived it—layer by layer—showing how the Lord can penetrate the core of the personality to bring healing to the inner person. The result is a story of victory in Christ through the operation of the Holy Spirit.

Those who read this story should be able to see how unhealthy is the denial of stress and sickness. They should also be able to see ways to start a personal crusade toward recovery lest the temptation to ignore symptoms become too strong. Mrs. Beggs is right: A decision to be released from the "dead hand of the past" is a matter of personal choice. Only then can the cycle of illness in the family be broken.

Raymond T. Brock, Ed.D.

Preface

Mary Beggs was not a stranger to me when the Lord brought us together to work on this book. She had attended the church in Texas where my husband pastored several years ago when all of us were in Bible college, preparing to be missionaries.

Mary was a delightfully warm person, always appearing to be on top of things. I had no idea she had walked such a rough road to attend Bible college.

Our paths have crossed only occasionally over the past twenty years. But when my husband was in Uganda with Jimmy and Mary Beggs for evangelism crusades several months ago, I felt compelled to join him. I found Mary in a "valley of decision" about the material in this book, and it was my privilege to walk with her through this valley. I was also there to help her deal with the pain and fear that were necessary to dredge up in order for her to tell her story.

Our hope is that every reader will become aware of the truth that with God's help they do have a choice in life's circumstances.

Colleen Tipton

Acknowledgments

To my friend, Colleen Tipton—who gave unselfishly of her time to help me relive the emotional pain of the first half of this story

To Mark and Dewey—for their input concerning my story

To my mother—for bringing me into the world

To my brothers and sisters—for being so much a part of my life

To my oldest brother Gene—who died while this book was being written

To my love, Jimmy—who encouraged me to write

Introduction

"Oh, no!" I cried as I grasped my left hand. "The diamond is gone from my wedding ring." I felt a sudden emptiness, an actual pain in my heart. I had worn that diamond for twenty-six years. My husband and I looked everywhere for it. We even took apart the sink drains and the water pump in the washing machine.

Five weeks later I was sitting at my desk in the hall, praying. At the end of the hallway was a glass-paned door that opened onto the patio. The cool, morning breeze was blowing from the open door and it was a beautiful day. But in spite of the clear, fresh air and brilliant sunshine, I was burdened in my spirit.

I was concerned about whether or not to write this book. I was also praying again about the loss of the diamond from my wedding ring. Amid a mixture of thoughts, I asked the Lord, *Am I really supposed to write this book? I don't want to tell this story—it tells too much about Mama and the pain my family suffered.*

My eyes were drawn to the bright sun shining on the tiled floor out on the veranda. I saw something silvery blue, glittering in the sun. My heart raced and I gasped. *No, it can't be!* But I knew a glitter like that had to be a diamond.

Wiping my tears away, I ran out onto the patio and picked up the stone. Sure enough, it was my diamond.

As I held it gently in my hands, the presence of Jesus was very near. I heard Him saying to my spirit, *Write the story. It will shine for my kingdom just like your diamond is still shining. I took care of the diamond when you thought it was gone forever, and I'll take care of you. Write the story.*

I was deeply moved. We had gone in and out of that door dozens of times during the past five weeks. Why was that diamond not swept away?

It hadn't been the dollar value of the diamond that concerned me. It was the fact that I had worn it all my married life—twenty-six years; it was a precious emblem of the love Jimmy and I have. Not only is the diamond still shining, but so is our marriage because of the Son.

I have shared in depth and in detail some of the joy and pain of our marriage through the years. Yes, we are ministers; we are missionaries. We dare to be honest because we know many other Christian marriages are hurting, and we want to encourage them.

I recall having lunch one day with a minister and his wife. During the course of the meal he referred to marriage problems: "We need to keep these things hidden," he declared, "or we will be stumbling blocks to our youth."

I felt sad. I believe it's better to let young people know some of our trials and pain. Then when a storm hits, they'll be encouraged to believe that they, too, can weather it.

Pure honesty spoken in love can bring healing to someone else. Having enough openness to say, "We know what it's like to hurt, and this is how we handled our problem," can be an encouragement.

If I have passed "through the valley of Baca [and made] it a well" (Psalm 84:6), then I will tell the next couple, whom the enemy would like to see destroyed, where cool refreshing water can be found.

In the heaviness of chaos and pain, Jesus kept my marriage. It could have been lost forever, but He kept it through an emotional, painful time that estranged Jimmy and me in the mid-years.

But we made the choice to fight for what was ours—a marriage sealed in heaven to be kept by our Lord and Savior, even in severe temptation. I know God's grace. With every temptation He will make a way to escape—when we choose to let Him.

Part One

1

The Promise

"Increasing knowledge results in increasing pain" (Ecclesiastes 1:18, NASB).

The green grass in the Great Rift Valley looked more luscious than ever. The haze that usually hid the sharpness of the distant trees and small hills was gone because of the morning shower.

My children, Suzan, age three, and Greg, age five, were searching earnestly for straw flowers that grew among the mossy rocks in this remote eighty-five-hundred-foot-high picnic site. The kids would run back to my husband, Jimmy, and me, present their gift of flowers, and then run away to find some more. It was a peaceful and beautiful day, and I felt pensive.

I looked behind me at the tall evergreens that were planted by German settlers in this part of East Africa. The gorgeous world God made was in harmony with the atmosphere of this place. World's End View—a perfect name for such a site. Somehow the cool, brisk breeze on this mountaintop with its exotic view increased the

17

emotions I was struggling with. A sadness settled over my spirit.

I turned to look at Jimmy. He was gazing out over the valley. The largest rift valley in the world, it stretches for hundreds of miles from north Africa down to southern Africa. This particular site in southern Tanzania was hypnotic. Nearby was a rain forest. Then just down the hill a few miles were gardens, and farther into the valley were plains where wild animals roamed.

Jimmy withdrew his eyes from gazing into the valley and looked at me. "You seem far away," he said. "What are you thinking about?" He covered the basket that had held our food. We were preparing to leave in a few minutes to go home, which was about twelve miles away.

"Oh, Jimmy, I should be the happiest person in the world. But at times, especially in the quiet of this gentle place, there's an ache inside. Will I ever get over the pain about Mama?"

We began talking about the emotional pain I had suffered ever since I was ten years old, when my mother had a nervous breakdown. The isolation we were enjoying here by the valley gave me the opportunity to talk with Jimmy about some of the memories that surfaced in my mind from time to time.

Jimmy and I had been married only six years. We had had both our children within three years' time, pastored in America, and completed the requirements for appointment as missionaries.

We loved what we were doing. Jimmy was a wonderful preacher. He was teaching in the Bible school in Mbeya, Tanzania, where we were serving our first term as missionaries.

Suzan and Greg brought vivacious joy to us. We spent a lot of time alone with our little family since fellowship with Americans was scarce in Tanzania. That day at the picnic when I shared some of the deep feelings I had as a result of my mother's problem was to be the first, and one of the few times over the years, that I would talk to Jimmy about it. I didn't know then that an emotional depression would come to me, too, at the age of thirty-nine—the same age my mother was when she had had her breakdown.

My emotional pain since childhood, which I was telling Jimmy about that day, had resulted from two separate areas. One was from the church that I had attended all during childhood, and the other was from my mother and the problems she had suffered.

I remember it like this:

ONE WINDY MARCH DAY Mama and I walked from the edge of town where we lived, to the church for the morning prayer meeting. I was ten years old. Mama always took me with her to these prayer meetings, and I loved going along. We stopped on an old wooden bridge with steel beams over the top of it. Mama looked up through the beams and into the sky rather sadly as she asked me, "Junie, if anything ever happens to me, you will help me, won't you?"

("Junie" was her nickname for me. I was born in late spring, and my dad called me June Bug. Mama had shortened it to Junie.)

"Mama, I will always help you with anything." It was a promise. But I couldn't imagine anything ever happening to her. She was Mama, and I had always depended on her.

We watched a fish swim out of the main stream and struggle to get off the big flat rock back into the flow. I wanted so badly to help that fish, but Mama said we had better keep going or we would be late.

After the prayer meeting, the women gathered in little clusters, talking to each other. Some were talking with Mama and others were whispering in a group by themselves. I was standing closer to the women who were not with Mama. The way they acted I knew they were talking about Mama.

"She's cracking up," whispered one.

"What could be the matter with her?" another asked. "The other day she said to me, 'He's a queer.' "

"Something's wrong with her," one said, "that she says such things about our pastor."

I stood there wondering, *What is Mama telling them that upsets them? What is she saying?* I wasn't sure what to do about the whispers, but at that moment a dark cloud settled on my world. I was scared of what I was feeling, and angry because it was my mother they were whispering about. I felt a chill come over me as I eased over to the red cannas that grew by the side of the church building and felt their smooth, thick leaves.

Mama mentioned that something might happen to her, I thought, *and the women are talking like something has happened already.*

A few minutes later Mama and I started home. Mama had a way with her—no matter what might be going on, she always sang. She took my hand in hers as we walked along and she sang what I had heard her sing hundreds of times: "Tell me the story of Jesus, / Write on my heart every word; / Tell me the story most precious, / Sweetest that ever was heard."

Maybe it's not the end of the world after all, I thought. *Things must not be so bad after all. Mama is singing like she always does. I love Mama and I know everything is going to be all right.*

My feeling of security was returning. As we stepped onto the old wooden bridge again, I skipped a little faster toward our house. It was a nice day, even though the sand was blowing a little and the sky was hazy. As Mama sang, I hummed with her.

A few days later I was talking to my older sister Nancy, and I asked her what *queer* meant. She explained that it was when men do bad things with one another.

Now I understood why the women were whispering and why Mama had looked so hurt and troubled. She believed our pastor was queer. (I later learned that Mama had discerned this while in prayer.) She had confided in one of the ladies who often prayed with her, and somehow word had reached the church leaders. Homosexuality was a terrible, almost unmentionable sin in a small town in 1950.

I loved my pastor and church very much, but I began to feel that the church was my enemy. People in the church were angry. The leaders of the church were outraged. People came to our house to argue with Mama and plead with her to put an end to the stories. Mama always sent us out of the room, but I could still hear what was being said, and I was frightened for her. I believed Mama, but I was confused at the way the church responded.

In response to the accusation, the pastor said piously, "You dear folk know this can't be true. The woman is sick."

Everywhere we went we heard talking and whispering about Mama. Some people were vicious, others judgmental, and a few simply amazed and heartbroken that Mama had voiced her ideas about the pastor.

My daddy had a temper. He met the pastor downtown and hit him in the face for abusing Mama. I knew this was wrong, but my loyalty to Mama was strong, and I was glad Daddy stuck up for her. When I saw the church people gang up on her, I knew I had a job to do. I had to help her. I had promised I would on that day we went to the prayer meeting.

Mama's devotion to church had made a deep and lasting impression on me. So when Sunday night came, the older kids and I got ready to go to church, just like always.

Mama said, "I don't think it's best, but you can go."

How can we not go? I wondered. Church was all we knew. It was our life. Of course we must go. So we all walked to church as usual. Mama was expecting her thirteenth baby any day and sometimes didn't go to church, even when Daddy or my brothers offered to take her in the car.

When we got to church one of the men I had known all my life and had high regard for met us at the door.

"You kids better not come in tonight," he said. "You can come later when things settle down." There was an exchange of words between him and my brother Forest. I can still see that man's face. He looked gray and sadder than anyone I'd ever seen.

I turned and sat down on the grassy lawn. I felt rejected by the church that I loved and even more rejected by the people and pastor I loved. Yet, I knew I still loved Jesus.

I felt the grass scratching my legs as I put my head in my arms and began to cry. I didn't understand it all and my brothers and sisters probably didn't either, but I knew it was agony to be on the outside looking in. Although the man at church had said we could come back, I knew he didn't really mean it. What would life be like without the church? I couldn't imagine.

As I put my hands to the ground to push myself up and follow my brothers and sisters home, a strange quietness settled inside of me. *Let them do what they want,* I thought. *I'm going to keep loving Jesus. And now I have to help Mama.* I walked slowly home that evening, home to Mama.

But Mama wasn't the same. She had changed during that awful weekend when the story came out. I remember the sequence of events: I had given Mama my promise; the women whispered; the church seemed to expel us; and finally the last baby came to live with us.

I adored baby Phyllis, just as I had Patsy, the little blonde-haired, blue-eyed baby before her. I had to take care of them a lot and didn't always do it willingly, but I loved them dearly.

One night, a short while after Phyllis was born, my world again seemed to fall apart. I heard the voices of Daddy and my brothers across the cotton field in front of our house calling, "Mama. Mama. Come home, Mama. Where are you, Mama?"

"Did you look in the pasture behind the house?" I heard Daddy ask my brother Forest.

"We have looked everywhere we know to look," Forest answered. I heard both anger and fear in his voice.

"She's got to be somewhere close," said Faith Hope, an older sister.

"Maaama! Come on, dadgummit!" I heard my brother Jackie cry, with a mixture of fear and what else, I didn't know.

Mama had run away into the blackness and I felt the horror of it as I kept going to the window to peek out: I was afraid of the darkness. I was afraid to go search for her, and I was afraid not to go.

"Stay in the house and watch the babies," Daddy said.

"Oh, Jesus, don't let the wolves get her. Bring her back, please," I prayed. "Is this what 'cracking up,' is Jesus? Is this what those women meant? God, help us all." I was crying inside as I mixed Phyllis' bottle, warming it in a pan on the stove. Suddenly I knew I really didn't like those women at the church anymore. Why did they have to stand and whisper about my mother anyway? I also knew hate was wrong, but I felt hate for all of them.

I kept wondering what was going to happen to all of us. I don't remember going to bed, but Mama was home the next morning. But she went to bed that day and didn't get up for many mornings.

Mama had a nervous breakdown in what they called the change of life. She was thirty-nine years old and had just given birth to her thirteenth baby. (She had a deep conviction that it was wrong not to have babies.) I could not undo

25

what was troubling her, but I had promised to help her. I went to her bedside. She felt so soft and tender as I touched her cheek.

"I love you, Mama," I said. "I'm sorry." Mama started to cry. I remembered the day we had gone to the prayer meeting and the feeling of the wooden bridge under my sandaled feet. I saw in my mind the hazy March sky with the dirt swirling in the breeze. I remembered again my promise to help Mama no matter what would happen to her. As I remembered the whispers of the women, I felt a strong desire to protect my mother. I didn't know how to do it, but I knew in my heart I *would* do it and would dare anyone to stop me.

Our expulsion from church and Mama's breakdown happened within a short time of each other. They seemed completely intertwined to me; I could not separate the two. I didn't know which hurt the most. The church had turned us out with their self-righteous attitudes and cold acceptance. Mama could not cope with this rejection either. It was too much for her, and she collapsed.

A number of years passed before the pastor was proven guilty. He was "caught" and put out of his Fellowship for being a homosexual. But in my childish mind, he had long been a traitor. The damage had already been done to our family, and there was no way to erase the wrongdoing.

God became my best friend during those difficult times, and I believed His miraculous power was at work in the daily affairs of my young life. One step at a time the Holy Spirit gave me the needed stamina to endure life. The nurturing years and encouragement Mama had given to me before her breakdown were vital to the choices I would make from then on. Should I give up or go on? Over and over I faced this choice as I dealt with painful situations.

2

Just Like Mama

"Train up a child . . ." (Proverbs 22:6, NASB).

I was always loyal to Mama. The memories I
have of her before her breakdown make me even
more loyal to her memory today. Her love and
knowledge of God built in me a desire to know
Him as she did.

My earliest memory of Mother's spiritual in-
fluence on my life goes back to when I was not
yet four. My daddy was drafted into the armed
services. He had nine children at that time, and
a man taken away from such a large family was
big news in our town. A reporter came to our
house to take pictures and write a story about
us. Talk about excitement!

One of my shoes was lost and everyone was
yelling. Someone said, "Mary's shoe is lost."

Mama, in her always-find-a-way voice, said,
"Well, we can borrow one of Damond's shoes."
He was the little boy who lived with his family
on the top floor of our two-story house.

My three-year-old heart rebelled. *I don't want
to wear that boy's shoes,* I thought. *I want my*

own. I also wanted to be in that picture, and the only way was to wear his shoes.

I can still see that picture of us. Mama had her hair in a pretty, smooth bun on the back of her head. The curls around her forehead were touched with silver. She had on a white dress; she looked beautiful. Daddy held the baby in his arms and the rest of us lined up where the photographer put us. It *was* big news for a man with nine children to be drafted: That picture was printed all over America.

Daddy chose to go into the Navy. After he was gone, Mama would gather us all into the living room of that big old framehouse every night and read a Scripture and pray for Daddy. All of us prayed together. My special place to pray was by the side of Mama's old trunk. She always had old metal trunks with wooden trim that she kept special things in. They seemed like part of the family. I remember those nights with warm but also sad feelings. We missed Daddy.

Finally, the government let Daddy come home because of his big family that needed him. He wanted to surprise Mama, so he didn't let us know he was coming. One day two of the older kids were walking down the street. Daddy was on the other side of the street. He pulled his hat down to keep them from recognizing him.

One of them said, "That looks like Daddy."

The other said, "Hey, yeah! It *is* him."

After another look they bolted for home.

29

"Daddy is coming! Daddy is coming!"

Mama started crying. She jumped up and in her excitement broke her big toe on the foot of a chair. But she kept on running to meet Daddy.

"Thank You, Jesus! Thank You, Jesus!" Mama said.

I knew even at that young age that those moments were really special for Mama and Daddy. I knew they loved each other. And I knew Jesus had brought Daddy home.

MAMA WAS ALWAYS FAITHFUL in taking us to church. Rain or shine, no matter what else was happening at our house, when church time came she had every one of the kids ready and headed down our street to church. An elderly neighbor, Mr. Honeycutt, was always sitting on his front porch. As Mama and her little troop went by, he would say, "There goes Ruby with her kids. You can set your clock by the sound of their footsteps going to church on Sunday morning."

When I was four and a half, my Sunday school teacher said, "Mary, you will memorize this poem for the play."

I grasped the little piece of paper in excitement and headed for the sanctuary.

"Mama, Mama, I have to learn this for the Christmas play. See?" I squealed as I handed the poem to her.

As soon as we got out of church, I started asking Mama to help me learn the poem. She promised she would. Every day I asked her. She kept promising, but Mama had young babies; it was difficult for her to take the time to help me.

Practice time came, and I still hadn't learned my part. When it was my turn to recite, I stood up. I was so upset because I didn't know my part that I started to cry. Our pastor came and put his arm around me and offered to help me after practice.

I raced home to Mama and said, "Mama, the pastor tried to help me learn my poem!" I didn't understand the look on her face, but she took time to see that I had learned my part by the next play practice.

My pastor patted me on the head and said, "You are a smart little girl, Mary."

I do believe that was the happiest Christmas I ever had. I had experienced my first feeling of accomplishment. This was also a time for spiritual growth. As I recited the lines

What can I give Him poor as I am?
If I were a shepherd, I would bring a lamb,
If I were a wise man, I would do my part,
So, what do I give Him? I give Him my heart,

I knew then that I loved Jesus and understood that Christmas was His birthday.

Babies kept coming to our house. Mother was busy but I knew she loved me dearly.

I loved Mama and always wanted to obey her and be near her. I was the sixth child, and I remember my brothers and sisters calling me

Mama's pet. It didn't really bother me, because I felt loved by Mama. I was always ready to do whatever I could for her.

Daddy worked hard and long, and often came home late. Mama postponed discipline until he got home, and someone usually got a spanking each night. I learned to fear the noises from the one who was in trouble when Daddy arrived. I don't remember feeling too afraid of him. It appeared to me if I stayed in good with Mama, then Daddy wouldn't bother me.

DURING THE SUMMER WHEN I WAS SIX years old, Mama led me to Jesus. I had always loved Jesus, but at that time I made a conscious decision to follow Him. Perhaps I had given Him my heart already at the Christmas program a year and a half earlier but didn't realize what was taking place. Anyway, the experience that summer was different.

My family had traveled to East Texas to gather crops. I was excited as we traveled. Daddy had made an enclosure for our pickup with windows and a back door. We kids piled in the back and I found a place by a window. I pressed my nose against the windowpane so I wouldn't miss one sight. The trees in this area were big and a luscious green. I liked this place; the big rivers fascinated me. After we arrived, Daddy took the shell off the back of the truck. I loved riding in the back with the wind blowing on my face.

After settling into the farmhouse we would

be living in for a few months, I heard Mama say, "Daddy, it's a long way to town."

The large town was about twelve miles from where we were, and in those days twelve miles was a long way to drive. If we were to go to church there, it would mean coming home late at night.

Mama and Daddy went to look for a place to worship. They found it. We would have Sunday night services in the old Whitewood Community Church about a mile from our temporary home. It had not been used for a long time.

We kids thought it was so much fun to get into the back of the pickup! The gravel crunched under the wheels as we pulled into the church-yard.

"All you kids sit near the front and be nice now," Mama said.

I hadn't realized Mama was going to be the preacher. She had invited people from miles around to come and worship, and come they did.

"I just couldn't live here and not have church," I heard Mama telling one of the ladies. That woman seemed to really admire what Mama was doing. My older brothers and sisters went to the front of the church and made a choir. Oh, how I adored and looked up to them! I looked over at Mama. She looked like an angel to me as she took her place at the front to preach.

Mama told us about Jesus dying for us and said that no matter how good we were we had to be saved to go live with Him. I knew I wanted to thank Him for dying for me.

I knew Mama loved Jesus and I wanted to love Him, too, and be like her.

"Jesus, forgive me. I want to love You all my life," I prayed. "Please save me now like Mama said You would. I want to go to heaven with You someday."

Acts 16:31 says, "Believe on the Lord Jesus Christ and thou shalt be saved," and it worked. Something happened then and there for me as I knelt by the old desktop chair that raised up and down. I had pulled it down and was crying into my arms as I talked to Jesus. Jesus had chosen me that night, and I had to follow Him. I felt all washed out and clean inside.

I didn't tell anyone at the time what had happened to me, but a few days later I said to Mama, "When you preached about Jesus the other night, I let Him save me." She hugged me and said something about her Junie loving Jesus just like Mama.

That was a marvelous summer for me. When it was over and the crops were gathered, we went back home. School had already started but I soon caught up with the other kids. One cool October day I ran all the way home with a slip of Big Chief tablet paper in my hand. Bursting into the house from school, I yelled, "Mama, Mama, look! I can print my name." I just knew she would be so happy to see what I had accomplished. Sure enough, I got a hug and a "Junie, I'm proud of you."

My world seemed quite all right with Mama's approval. Mama motivated me with her approval. What Mama loved, I loved. I knew she loved the Bible, God's Word, and so I learned all the books of the Bible and recited them at children's church. In some respects I was doing what pleased Mama, yet at the same time my choices gave me feelings of contentment and satisfaction.

The years before Mama's breakdown were uplifting, but the years afterwards brought much pain. Not knowing how to deal with the hurt, I decided to hide my inner feelings. The Mama I knew had changed, and as a child, I didn't understand it or know how to deal with the situation.

3

The Hiding Game

"Even in laughter the heart may be in pain"
(Proverbs 14:13, NASB).

I used to love to play hide-and-seek late into the night of a hot West Texas summer. I would become totally involved; sweat running down my hairline, I would run into home base yelling with all my strength, "Free, free!" The person who got caught was always "It." I revelled in getting in free because that proved my ability to stay hidden the longest. And then I didn't have to be "It," or be singled out. I loved this hiding game.

Another hiding game I was good at was concealing the pain and inadequacy I felt after my mother's nervous breakdown. The first time I can remember trying to hide my home situation was in third grade health class. We were all expected to wear clean clothes and have our nails clean and our hair combed. My mother had been sick in bed for weeks. On this particular school morning I had quickly combed my hair, but hadn't thought about my nails. My dress was dirty when I left home that morning to walk two miles to school, and I had forgotten that it was health-check day. White stars meant passing; gold ones meant excellent.

I felt that I wasn't clean, but I desperately wanted approval. I was ashamed, but I didn't want my teacher to know. I frantically began to clean my nails by passing each one through my teeth, biting away the dirt of yesterday's mud pies. I borrowed a comb and tried to get out the tangles I had missed earlier in the morning. There was little I could do about the dress.

Maybe if I smile she won't know how scared I really am of failing health check this morning, I thought.

The teacher picked up my hand and carefully examined it. I boldly looked her in the face and smiled. My heart was racing like the water in the creek where we played near our house. *Accept me,* I pleaded silently. She stood there looking at me. I didn't know how to read her reaction but the smile worked. She said, "It will do for a white star today. Tomorrow, get your mother to help you, and be sure you wear a clean dress."

I felt every bit the small, scared girl that I was, from a home where a mother was too sick to know if I was clean or not. After that day I tried to remember health check and to never get caught again. I felt like the crawfish my brothers and sisters and I were always catching in the creek. Sometimes they backed away out of reach. I had backed out of that teacher's way and had gone on down the stream of life with a smile. I had gotten in free. I would not forget this experience of hiding my feelings and smiling.

I trusted God to help me daily, but I was setting some patterns that would lead to greater pain. Hiding my true emotions and feelings only caused the problem to increase. Not knowing how to be honest and vulnerable, I continued to appear confident and in control—but I was hurting on the inside. Hiding became such a habit that I couldn't distinguish the difference between the real me and the person I wanted to be. Yet, at the time, I felt this was the only way I could cope.

IN THE FALL WE PULLED COTTON from the time the dew was dry in the morning until sunset. Oh, how hot the sun was! I would stand to straighten my back in the afternoon when the going would get the hardest. Often I saw the school bus go by.

"Daddy, when do I get to start back to school?" I would ask.

He replied with a sad, slow smile, "When the best of the pulling is over, June Bug." That seemed like forever.

But those days in the cotton fields gave me some of my happiest family memories. Once, one of my older brothers stepped on a rabbit's nest. The rabbit jumped straight into the air. Someone yelled, "Chunk 'im." The hard green bolls started flying from all directions. One well-aimed boll hit the rabbit in the head with a thud. Stunned, the rabbit fell on its face but quickly regained its senses and continued its frantic flight. We all laughed and slapped our thighs as we each told our version of the story. At times like these we forgot the hot sun and our aching backs.

Usually I didn't start back to school until the last of October or first of November. As a result, I had a very poor foundation in elementary school, and I had to hide my embarrassment of being behind. I felt left out. I was behind in all my workbooks. I didn't know the previous spelling list. I worked hard to catch up, and knots came to my stomach when I looked at my notebooks. Discouragement would grip me.

Yet, something deep down inside would rise within me and I would plunge into the work, striving to accomplish my assignments. I felt unworthy and scared in the classroom. Still, I decided to work hard, and I made good grades.

One day in seventh grade the students started asking for information about their grades from the English teacher.

"Mrs. Blake," I said as I raised my hand, "I would like to know about my work in your class, too."

"Mary, you have had a poor foundation, but you are determined, and you try hard. I don't doubt you will be what you choose to be."

That dear lady gave my morale the boost it needed. She filled a need Mama hadn't been able to meet for me since she had become ill. I didn't need to hide things with Mrs. Blake. She understood. In her room I could be honest.

Although I overcame my struggle with school, I didn't have the spiritual maturity I needed to handle the attitudes of many Christians who knew about Mama's depression. This caused a deep ache inside me.

Not everyone said what they thought to my face, but I heard many things secondhand.

"If she would get right with God, that problem would go away."

"This can't be anything but demonic."

"What a shame . . . and with all those kids."

In response, I smiled, never letting anyone know how much their condemning silence or comments affected me. I simply hid from them all. I loved my mother, and I smiled on the outside to protect her, as well as myself, from pain.

Even as I write these words of judgment and accusation that were said about Mama, I cringe. I have to admit that the old anger still wants to rise toward those people. I am learning to handle the anger that is sometimes a result of pain. I ask God to take it from me, then my heart relaxes and I rest in Him.

Sometimes pain caused by Christians is more intense than other pain because we expect better treatment from Christians. I'm grateful there are different types of church people. As I was growing up, the dear, sweet ones who shook my hand, patted my arm, and smiled into my eyes are the ones I remember with gratitude. They gave me courage to keep choosing to cope by persevering.

4

Substitute Mother

"Remember also your Creator in the days of your youth" (Ecclesiastes 12:1, NASB.)

Mama had been sickly ever since her nervous breakdown. Sometimes she would lie in bed for days, not talking or doing anything. Other times she would sit and talk to us.

When I was fourteen years old I had to become substitute mother to six younger brothers and sisters. (One of my younger brothers died when I was just a toddler.) My sister just older than I, who had been taking care of things, got married, so I was next in line to take over household chores. This meant that on days Mama was not able to manage, I was in charge of the house, the little kids, and preparing meals.

I came home from school one cold winter day and saw Mama writing on some lined paper. I thought she might be coming out of the depression. I tried to get her to talk to me, but she would only look blankly at me and keep writing. Daddy tried to get her to go to bed late that evening, but she wouldn't respond. Finally, he got angry and grabbed the paper she was writing on and started to read. He wilted—if a heart-broken man can wilt any more than he already had. His face looked ashen. He told me he was going to bed.

The next morning when I got up, Mama was still writing. The pages were all neatly stacked on the table beside her. She had not even slept. I silently prayed, *I'm sure glad I know you, Lord. I would hate to be in this alone.* Maybe the writing was an outlet for Mama, but it was terrible for the rest of us.

Sometimes we kids really got embarrassed by Mama's writing. She would send notes to school with us for principals and teachers. Some of my brothers and sisters threw them away. Mama wrote long letters to the colleges and newspaper editors of America. However, many of these letters never made it to the post office to be weighed for postage. But letters for teachers didn't have to be weighed for postage, so Mama mailed them from the front porch.

As she kept writing, Mama also got bolder in talking and sharing her visions. Mama wrote frequently for about three years. She wrote truth mixed with fantasies, and she began to live the fantasies.

"Junie, someday the president of the United States will call me to come preach on television and rid America of Communism."

She kept a set of clothes in one of her old

trunks for this occasion, the same metal trunks with the wood trim that I had knelt by to pray for Daddy when he had been drafted.

"I hear you, Mama," I would reply. I didn't argue with her. I agreed with her so she wouldn't get hurt or angry.

Mama had a preoccupation with Communism. I remember as a young girl I felt such empathy with her about this burden. When Joseph Stalin died I was in the sixth grade. The news came over the radio and I rushed to Mama's bed to tell her. "Mama, Mama, the Communisms' (as I called it) leader just died. Now they can't come and take America. They're finished in the whole world, reckon?"

She sadly explained, "Junie, they will get another man, and he might be even meaner."

Over the years Mama started helping some in the house again. Then she would revert and have days of fantasy.

The further away Mama drifted from us, the more I depended on church and prayer. They gave me my main strength. Daddy had started taking us children to a church across town from our old one. It was a new church that had started when an oil boom brought new people into the community.

At the new church I would go to the altar and talk to Jesus. He was my Helper. I also talked to myself, especially when I was tired or discouraged. My real strength in "self-talking"

44

came from God. (I think they were what would be called conversational prayers today.)

"God, I have lots to do today. I know You'll help me."

"Lord, they don't believe I'm really going to go to college. Sometimes I feel scared. I don't have the money. Please give me the courage, Jesus."

"God, Mama has cried all day. All I ask is just help us. Help us all."

MY FIRST YEAR IN HIGH SCHOOL was my toughest. I was substitute mother, and I worried about Mama. Something that helped my job as substitute mother was my homemaking class: We talked about schedules and running a home. I tried to apply the things I learned to what I had to do at home.

I decided the first thing I needed was a system, one like Miss Perriman talked about in class. I made myself a schedule—and it worked.

"You and I are going to make it, God; we're going to make it."

Yet, the work was still hard, and I felt so alone.

Every morning I got up early and fixed gravy and bread or toast and jelly. My brothers and sisters just younger than me helped with getting the smallest kids ready for school. I learned to prepare some meals the night before, like cooking beans.

If Mama was too depressed to get up, the

youngest children played near her bed while we were at school. On other days the smaller boys stayed home from school to help watch the two youngest girls.

I never knew what a day would hold. Some days Mama talked to us and told us what things needed to be done. Other days she would stay in bed and cry or sleep all day. The youngest children didn't know Mama in any other way and never asked any questions. I could take Mama's crying better than I could the blank stares. That's when I felt the most left out and alone with the children and the chores.

After I was ready for school each day, I lectured the kids before leaving them. To Patsy, next to the youngest, I said, "Keep the baby in the house if it is cold. Stay out of the road if you go outside."

In spite of the obstacles I usually headed for school with a happy spirit. Most nights after supper was over, I did my homework, and I don't remember ever not having it done for school the next day. I liked school and made good grades.

Down the street from where we lived was the old help-yourself laundry. Once a week I gathered up all the dirty clothes and put them in a little red wagon. With my little brother Alton pushing and me pulling, we got the wagon across the street and up the road to the little gray stucco building.

Mama had taught me how to separate the colored clothes from the whites and lights; I took pride in doing the laundry right, which included the use of bluing. I liked the feel of the water running over my hands and seeing things come out bright and clean. All of us kids had to help hang the clothes out, and Bobbie and I divided the ironing between us.

When Mama was having a good day, the younger kids would gather around her and stay close. This made it easier for me to make sure the work in the house was done. Each child had a job to do and if he didn't get it finished, I threatened to tell Daddy. That usually worked because Daddy's punishment was harsh. But his spirit seemed to be mellowing with Mama's depression; he became more and more gentle with all of us.

Most of the time I spanked the kids myself, which made me feel very bad. They would cry and scream, "I hate you! I wish you were dead!"

I prayed, "God, I know sometimes I'm not very spiritual, but please help me." The memories of giving those spankings were painful to me for many years.

I seldom dated, but one night I met a boy at a church youth rally—and loved him immediately. As he sang and played his guitar, I was spellbound. How could anyone sing so beautifully, look so handsome, and be a neat Christian all in one bundle?

If I had not already felt God calling me to preach and to be a missionary—which would require college—perhaps I would have married this boy. But when I learned that he had quit school, I wouldn't allow myself to get too involved: I loved him from a distance. My little sisters and I used to sing a song about him and me. My friends knew I loved him.

Later, he and his parents moved north, about five states away. That seemed as far as the North Pole to me. He wrote and asked me to wait for him. Taking his letter, I went to the room I shared with my sisters, fighting hard not to cry. I wrote back to him, explaining the call of God on my life to be a missionary. Writing that letter was difficult, but I knew I had made the right decision.

Choosing God's call over my love for this boy gave me spiritual strength like I had never known. In English class a few days later, I wrote a poem about my preaching and missions call:

FOLLOWING HIM

I heard a sound far off,
It was so loud and yet so soft.

It seemed to beckon me near,
And to go to it . . . I have no fear.

The call rings out to follow Him,
I cannot let the vision dim.

Forsaking all, if the case may be,
To know my Master is pleased with me.

So as you see the call I've heard,
Making my eyes with tears be blurred.

"Follow me," said Jesus Christ to John,
So shall I . . . 'till His will be done.

I began to make friends more and more with young married women. Their friendships helped me release some stress from home, but sometimes they also gave me problems.

Lannie, a married girl just five years older than I was, came by the house one day. I was waxing the floor. Rather bossy and outspoken, Lannie said, "Mary, you should get out more. Why do you do all this stuff with your mama sitting in that chair? You're going to ruin your life."

Mama said, "I worked hard on this floor today, Lannie."

I desperately wanted to protect Mama. I sensed that she couldn't stop what she was doing, but I was crushed. She had not moved from her chair all day.

There was an awkward silence, and then Lannie asked me to go get a hamburger with her. On the way to the drive-in, we talked about other things, and I thought Lannie was going to overlook what Mama had said. But just as I started to take a bite of hamburger, she said, "Something should be done about your mother, Mary. She is crazy, you know."

I stiffened. I slowly laid down the hamburger and said in a whisper, "Take me home." I felt like Lannie had just slapped me. I sat staring out the car window all the way back home. No

one was going to hurt Mama if I had my way—
I remembered my promise to her on the old
bridge when I was ten. I never confided in Lannie again.

Day after day, Mama sat for hours without
getting up or moving. One day Patsy, with a
puzzled look said to me, "Junie, Mama can write
but she can't hear, can she? Why is Mama like
this? Why can't we get her ears fixed, Junie?"

I had become so used to the little kids talking
to Mother, patting her cheek, and trying to get
her attention that I didn't realize how they might
be feeling. Patsy had simply decided Mama
couldn't hear.

It made me angry because I shared the little
girl's confusion. I was angry at Mama for being
sick and at Daddy for not getting her any help.
Going to my room to pray, I took a songbook. I
turned to "I Must Tell Jesus" and started singing.

I must tell Jesus all of my trials;
I cannot bear these burdens alone. . . .

I must tell Jesus!
I must tell Jesus!
. . . Jesus can help me,
Jesus alone.

The anger finally lifted. It was unusual for
me to feel so angry. Most of the time I just hid
my feelings and declared, "God, I'll make it!"

One of my younger sisters, Bobbie Ann, didn't

like school. During high school she met a really nice boy and fell in love. In just a few months they wanted to get married. I was heartsick. This would be my third sister to marry as a teenager.

I wanted to beg her, *Don't marry. Stay with me. We can go to college together.* As we were standing in the vestibule of the church at the wedding, I whispered, "Not too late to change your mind." The pastor's son stepped up and said, "Leave her alone. She can marry if she likes." I felt guilty, and hushed.

At home after the wedding, I made the family some French fries and iced tea. As we all sat around the table without Bobbie Ann, tears began to roll down my cheeks. I had wanted her to stay at home. I brushed away the tears and got up from the table. Taking my tea, I went out under the big tree in our backyard and continued to cry. Something took place inside of me that day. A new kind of determination rose up as I promised myself, *Whatever it takes, I won't marry. I will graduate from high school first and then go to college.*

I was afraid to let my family see me cry. I didn't want them to think I was weak and couldn't handle the home situation. I did feel free to cry at church because it seemed that Jesus understood. He would let me cry for a while and then wipe away my tears and give me strength to go on. It would be some twenty-five years before I learned to have a good healthy cry.

At a missionary service in our church when I was fourteen years old, I heard a missionary from Africa speak. I can still see that missionary standing there telling us about the people in Africa, and that night I felt God drawing me toward missionary work on that continent. My heart ached for those people who didn't know Jesus.

God gave me a quiet faith to know I would reach Africa and love those people through His Son, Jesus Christ. I accepted the challenge He gave me to reach others, and I began promoting missions in our church youth group (of which I was the president). But I didn't tell anyone right away of my call to Africa.

To reach my goal of being a missionary, I knew I would have to finish high school and go on to college, which would go against the school dropout pattern practiced by most of the girls I knew. To reach my long-term goals, I practiced meeting short-term ones. No matter how tired I was, I did my homework and kept up my classwork. And I talked to God often, "Thanks for the A that I got on my paper. I knew You would help me."

My missions call was confirmed as I read missions stories and heard missionaries speak. I prayed every day about my desire to reach Africa, and I sought paths that would lead me there. My church was my social and spiritual reinforcement.

On her good days, Mama encouraged me spiritually. When she learned I was president of the youth group, she always wanted to be sure I was in church.

"Junie, preach," she told me. "Do what you can. The future will hold many changes for the church. Eventually, people will try to take prayer out of our schools." (Less than ten years later Madalyn Murray would start the legal battle that would do just that.)

Being youth leader opened up a whole new world for me. My pastor told the neighboring pastor in Coahoma about my speaking ability. The pastor in Coahoma invited me to come and speak at his church. Mama really wanted me to go.

While I was gone, Daddy watched the kids. One of the youth sponsors drove me to Coahoma. I started getting invitations to speak at other churches regularly. My pastor usually arranged for someone to take me. I was glad to have a pastor like him who believed in me.

Later, I was invited to come back to Coahoma and preach a two-week youth crusade. It was my first long crusade. I studied the Bible every day and spoke about twenty minutes each night. While I was there, I decided I wanted to see a vision of Jesus. I had heard a man talk about having seen Him, and I thought this would be marvelous. Thinking it would give me strength,

I went to the church during the day as usual to pray and this time asked Jesus to let me see Him in a vision.

On each side of the altar was a door opening into two different rooms. Suddenly, the wind blew one of the doors open. On the wall in the room was a picture of Jesus. I jumped, startled. The wind, the door, and the picture all frightened me. Quickly I left the altar and went outside. Very shaken, I decided to leave the visions to others and just do my Bible study and prayer.

When I spoke, most of my messages ran along the line of choosing a goal in life and having faith to work toward that goal. I encouraged youth to accept Christ, to follow Him, and to learn from their own personal experience with Him who they were and where they were going in life. It's understandable that this was often my theme, for I was in the midst of God's proving His strength and help to me in my everyday life.

The time for my high school graduation was nearing. For the past year Mama had been doing a little better. She had gone through a lot of stages in her illness. At first, she stayed in bed for weeks and weeks with no will to live. Then she spent days crying and staring. Later she wrote constantly.

With the uncertainty of what Mama would be like I was concerned about graduation and how she would act. She had talked to me so much about how Communism was hidden in the schools and government and about her desire to speak to the nation that I had a fear of what she would do if she attended my graduation.

The five younger kids still at home were excited about my getting to graduate. Daddy said he would drive them and Mama over to the auditorium. I rode with my girlfriend because we had to be there early.

As we put on our caps and gowns, I felt both elated and sad. The seniors were all yelling, playing, and talking about what they were going to do after the exercises. *God, just let Mama be all right until this is over*, I prayed.

Standing with my row, after the last person had been through the line, I started crying. *Thank You, Jesus. You and I made it, and I'm grateful to you.*

The girl next to me shook my shoulder and said, "Hey, don't cry! Be happy! This is a happy time."

How could I ever explain that these were tears of thanksgiving? I had finally graduated, and Mama had gotten through the ceremony without doing anything to embarrass me.

Daddy seldom showed tenderness, but he did that night.

Mama said, "Junie, I'm proud of you."

I was tired, relieved, and glad. I had graduated and with God's help accomplished my first big goal. I went home and slept soundly.

5

Together We Can

"Bear one another's burdens, and thus fulfill the law of Christ" (Galatians 6:2, NASB).

"These are my boys," said Mrs. Beggs, pointing to four photographs on the wall as she showed me to her neat sitting room.

"Wow!" I said out loud. They all looked so nice.

"You say you're a senior?" she asked, looking at me.

I nodded.

"Well, that's nice. Now you make yourself at home. I'm going to see about my bread. Pops and the boys will be here soon from San Angelo. They went to buy college clothes. My, clothes are expensive these days," she sighed, heading for the kitchen.

It was a winter weekend and I was in Big Lake, Texas, to hold a youth crusade in the Beggs' church. A few hours later I met Jimmy.

In traveling and being in pastors' homes, I had met many sons, but Jimmy was different. I was attracted to him immediately. He was a sophomore in college and I was a senior in high school. My first thought was, *Someone will claim him before I ever get there*. Fortunately, I had already made application to the same college.

"Mary, would you come again for a meeting this summer?" Rev. Beggs asked at the close of the weekend. "This time I'd like to have you stay for two weeks."

When graduation was over, I boarded the bus for the Beggs' home again. Riding along, I remembered Jimmy mentioning that he might not come home for the summer. He had a good campus job and didn't want to lose it. *Oh, I hope he will be there*, I kept thinking. He had been on my mind a lot, and I hoped we would meet again.

That summer Jimmy *was* home, and he stayed the first two weekends of the crusade. I had formed the habit of praying about everything in my life, and during those two weeks I asked the Lord—if it was in His plan—to let Jimmy ask me to write to him. I had learned that Jimmy, too, was planning to be a missionary. Falling in love with a man who also had a missions call was moving toward my goal, I thought.

Time in the Beggs' home was nearing an end. Jimmy had packed to return to college, and his parents walked outside to say good-bye to Jimmy and his two brothers, who were also in college. I waited in the house. Sitting on the couch, I thought, *Oh, no. He's leaving and he hasn't said a word about our corresponding. I guess it wasn't meant to be. And I like him so much.*

57

Suddenly, Jimmy appeared from a side door. He had left the group and come back into the house. He sat down beside me and started talking. I was swinging my shoe from the end of my foot. With a wonderful smile he reached down, took my shoe, and wrote his name on it.

"I'd like to write to you," he said. "Think you could manage that?"

I looked into Jimmy's blue eyes, smiled back, and said, "Yes." I was bursting with excitement.

Only a few letters passed between us until I learned that he, too, was planning on being a missionary to Africa. After he knew our goals were the same, Jimmy wrote me two letters a day. My dream was coming true. I had no doubts about us being able to form a good relationship. I then chose to let down my guard and fall deeply in love.

"JUNIE, DO YOU REALLY HAVE TO go away from us?" asked Patsy, who loved wearing my high heels. "And are you taking all your shoes?"

"Yeah, she has to have them to do her preaching," said Phyllis, the youngest.

Though it was difficult, I was finally making the break from home to go away to college. I felt excited, but hated leaving my little sisters and brothers. I left feeling guilty. Daddy got angry with me, and I felt rejected by him. But I knew this was how Daddy handled his frustrations; this was his way of letting me go.

When I reached the campus of Southwestern

Bible College I was elated. The glorious day had finally arrived. Stepping into the reception area of the girls' dorm I felt at home immediately. I was a college student.

"You are most welcome here, Mary," said Mom Kelly, the dorm mother.

I thought about home where my brother Forest was looking after Mama and the family. He had moved back to our hometown and had encouraged me to go to college.

"Go on, Mary. You could stay home another ten years and still not fix things. You would only miss doing what you feel God has called you to do."

I was free from a long, sad burden. Working every afternoon and on Saturdays in college was easy compared to the load I had carried at home. I was also finally free to be a teenager at nineteen.

After only two months on campus, I was chosen Miss Southwestern. This was one of the greatest surprises of my life, but I believe the students voted for me because I reached out to them. There was not a student on campus that I was not interested in. I cared for them all. I could sense the pain that some students were dealing with the moment we met. Perhaps it was because of my own pain that I could reach out to them. As a result, many students talked to me, and I encouraged them to do so. Although I listened to everyone else's problems, I didn't share my own.

Jimmy was the only one who had any idea of my background, and to him I confided just enough, but not too much. I was bound to a silent vow to protect Mama. If I told others about her, I would be a traitor. When any reference was made to my mother, I said only good things about her.

God again had answered my prayer. I had reached another goal with God's help. I was attending college and was in love with a man who shared my dream of being a missionary.

Many times I stood by my window on the second floor of the girls' dorm and watched for Jimmy to come out the front door of the boys' dorm. My heart sang, *He is coming to me. He's coming to me.* We were so happy and so in love.

I stood there and watched him as long as I could and then made a dash down the stairs where we always met to go to the cafeteria for our meals. I worshipped Jimmy.

I needed Jimmy's quiet stability; he needed my spontaneity. One night after a social we tried to sneak a kiss behind a shrub. Just about the time we were embracing, a pebble hit Jimmy's ankle. A little boy's voice, none other than a professor's son, cried out, "Someone's in that bush, Dad." I started to make a mad flight to the dorm. Jimmy grabbed me and whispered, "Be quiet. They'll go away." My spontaneity had almost got us caught. His deliberate thinking saved us from reprimand.

I am amazed when I recall those wonderful

days of courtship Jimmy and I had. Growing up, I had seen the pain in Mama and Daddy's relationship and vowed to myself, *If I ever get married, I will never hurt my husband. I'll meet him at the door with a kiss and he will never hear a negative word from me toward him.* I kept that vow for many years. But I handled my relationship with Jimmy as I had handled Mama, by not confronting him when we misunderstood each other.

Jimmy studied hard, often late into the night. Often he was very tired. One day he hurt his back on his job while lifting heavy furniture. The pain caused him to be very irritable. Such pressures put a strain on our relationship and his sharpness with me sometimes hurt me deeply. Yet, I would not tell him. Instead, I talked about the situation with his brother.

"Talk to him, Mary," he said.

I said I would, but I couldn't bear to let Jimmy know what I was really thinking. I was afraid I might hurt him.

Jimmy's good points were so many that the few things that bothered me were easy to bury.

I knew Jimmy needed me badly. And I liked to be needed. One day we were sitting in our favorite restaurant where we had gone for a Coke. Jimmy seemed much quieter than usual.

"What's wrong?" I asked.

He shook his head slowly and sadly. With tears in his eyes, he said, "I can't preach. I just can't do it. I'm too shy and it's so painful for me."

These words were probably the greatest challenge I had received in my life.

"Oh, Jimmy!" I said. "Of course you can. Together we can. Jimmy, you will be a great preacher."

That day I chose to become to Jimmy what I had been to Mama. I would help him hide his pain. I was totally committed to him.

We had dated for two and a half years. I had told Jimmy some things about Mama's situation. The first time he came to our home he saw a part of Mama I had hoped he wouldn't have to see.

Later, when we were alone, Jimmy said, "Mary, your mother showed me her special clothes from the trunks."

I looked down at the floor.

"Don't worry about it; I understand. She seems like such a good woman in other areas." He took my hands and I looked into his face. I realized he really did understand and accept her. Jimmy had seen the situation and loved me in spite of it.

Soon after Jimmy's graduation from college, we married. I married two years sooner than I had planned when I was younger, because Jimmy needed me. I remembered my vow not to ever hurt my husband. I admired and respected Jimmy, which made it even harder to let him know any negative feelings I had about him. I didn't realize that my protection of Mama had now been transferred to Jimmy.

Jimmy and I were a team, never out of each other's sight.

Jimmy accepted my ministry and depended on me. I allowed him the leadership as pastor even though I was a minister, too, and I took on the role of pastor's wife. I watched him grow in his ministry, and my greatest pleasure was the gratitude I received from him for my participation. When he would say, "Thanks, Mary. Your spirit and encouragement helped me in the service today," I felt fulfilled and happy.

Jimmy had his own difficulties expressing his feelings toward me as a woman, but neither of us realized it at the time. I gained affirmation from him only in the area of ministry. And since we shared the ministry, his approval gave me all the support I needed the first fifteen years of our life together.

AFTER ALL THE HELP I HAD GIVEN MAMA with her children, I was sure I wanted to wait five years to have a baby. But our wonderful blue-eyed baby, Greg, was born the first year. Now I had the roles of both mother and pastor's wife. We completed the pastoral years required for missions appointment and then made application for service in Africa. Nine months later we were accepted, and the following nine months were spent in making preparations to go.

During our itineration for missionary work, we made several visits home to see my family. Sometimes Mama was completely rational, but other times she was lost in her world of conquering Communism. One thing I remember on one of our visits was when she held our son Greg.

"Daddy," she said to my father, "they will take Greg all the way to Africa, and I may never see him again." I slipped into the next room and cried. I was carrying another baby at the time.

When Greg was almost three, our darling little Suzan joined us. She was a quiet, beautiful, dark-haired girl. We loved our babies. We had a son and a daughter. What more could we ask for?

6
Grief Without Tears

"There is a time . . . to weep" (Ecclesiastes 3:1,4, NIV).

"Pita hapa. Pita hapa," the ground steward-ess said and pointed to the immigrations officer.

"Is the babies on the mutha's passporti?" he asked. I smiled at the first African English I had heard. Neither Jimmy nor I, arriving for our first term of missionary service in Africa, had expected the accent to be so strong.

Half an hour later I was in the National Air-port lounge of Dar es Salaam, the capital* of Tanzania, East Africa. The black night and un-familiar sounds gave me an eerie feeling. I thought, *So this is deep, dark Africa. It has been eleven years since I first thought of Africa, and now here I am with my own family.*

The missionaries we were to work with were not there to meet us at the airport, so Jimmy was phoning them. He had trouble with the pay

---

*Dodoma, more centrally located, has since become the capital.

phone, which was complicated, and he could find only one man who could speak some English.

Our plane had been the last one in, and the airport had closed immediately after its landing. Every light went out except a dim one in front.

Overcome with fatigue, I sat down on the luggage with three-month-old Suzan in my arms. The flight across the ocean had been long. Three-year-old Greg was happy to be off the plane and was throwing rocks into the darkness, exploring his new surroundings.

An old man, an airport employee, sat down near me to reassure me. *"Haraka, haraka. Chelewa sana,"* he kept saying.

"I'm very sorry," I replied, feeling embarrassed at being unable to understand him. Later I learned he was saying, "Hurry! Very late, your friend." To this day I have a very warm feeling for that old gentleman who stayed near me and my babies upon my first coming to Africa. He walked away into the darkness only after our missionary hosts arrived.

I was nursing Suzan and felt thankful she had good, warm milk. Emotionally, I felt as if I had walked every step of the ten thousand miles to reach this place. Striving to reach my goal to be a missionary in Africa had taken determination, but I had finally fulfilled another goal.

We learned Swahili, an official language of Tanzania, quickly and efficiently. Within a year we both had passed the language test, proving our ability to read and write Swahili fluently. I had studied at home on my own because of the children, and it was worth every effort.

For twenty-one years I would use that language while working with African women, teaching them homemaking, hygiene, the Word of God, and how to be leaders of women's groups in their churches. I was able to start, through a pyramid method of teaching leaders, hundreds of women's prayer groups in those years. I would also write a handbook for leaders, teaching them the hows and whys of church women's groups.

Jimmy and I both were leaders in ministry and loved it. We were so busy with others, though, we did not realize what our own needs were. We only began to discover them that day, about three years after we had arrived in Africa, when we picnicked at World's End View and I brought up the pain of my childhood. Tragically, though, I didn't continue this kind of sharing with Jimmy.

When I would be open about one painful matter, other matters of pain would make themselves felt. My vow to protect and help Jimmy caused me to stop short of honest communication. And his sharing had not continued after that day during our courtship when he had revealed his feelings of inadequacy as a preacher.

During my first four and a half year term in Africa (1964–1969), Mama had written me a letter. "You are no longer my little girl, Junie, not if you could betray me this much."

I had talked to someone I trusted about Mama's problem, hoping that person could get her to go to a doctor. But Mama found out and was deeply offended. About the same time I started receiving Mama's letters venting her anger about my betrayal, Suzan was extremely ill and often had a fever as high as 104 degrees. She had been born with malfunctions of her bladder and urinary tract. Doctors said only surgery would correct the problem.

In the midst of struggling with Suzan's serious illness and Mama's emotional outburst, I became discouraged. For the first time, my determination to be strong started to weaken. Then I came across the book *They Speak With Other Tongues*, by John Sherrill.

I had prayed in the Spirit since I was eleven years old, but this book enriched my spiritual prayer life. I read it straight through, fell on my knees in my bedroom, and wept before God. A new flow of the Holy Spirit surged through me. I allowed His love and Spirit to revitalize my strength. My new appreciation for the gift of the Holy Spirit, which I had begun to take for granted, gave me moral, spiritual, and even physical strength. I made a choice then to keep running the race. It was as though I had been rebaptized in the Holy Spirit. My prayer language became more meaningful to me than ever before. God met my need—new courage for Mama and my sick baby.

We lived in Africa for four-year periods, and every fifth year we went stateside for one year. One of those furloughs back to America, 1973–1974, was especially difficult. Before this furlough, my older sisters started writing that Mama was well.

"Mary, she cleans house and cooks for Daddy. She sings like she used to and never talks about her fantasies anymore. She loves her life now. She has a clear mind. You will love the way things are with her when you get home," they wrote.

Mama well! I was both glad and awed. Mama's letters to me were different too. She sounded happy like she was when I was a little girl. She spoke of taking care of Daddy and seemed excited about me coming home.

Because of my sisters' letters, I had tremendous hope of seeing Mama well again. I wanted to explain why I had tried to get help for her and bring healing between us. So it was a shock too deep to express when November 11, 1973—only six days before we were to board British Airways from Nairobi, Kenya, en route to Texas to see Mama—I received a phone call.

"Mary," my brother Forest said, "Mama died suddenly an hour ago. Can you come home right away?"

I couldn't comprehend the fact that she was really gone. Even though my family said she had been well, I thought she would never understand that I didn't hurt her intentionally or maliciously by trying to get her help. I was afraid my one letter of explanation and apology to her was not enough. *I was supposed to protect her, not let her die*, I thought. Now she was gone forever. I knew she would rise in the Resurrection according to the Bible. Emotionally, however, she was gone from me forever.

I didn't cry. I couldn't. I had taught myself that pain connected with Mama should not be acknowledged. I had talked to Jimmy in the past about some of my feelings toward Mama, but my emotions surrounding her death could not be expressed, even to him.

"Mary, oh, Mary," my sister-in-law cried out as I stepped off the plane in Texas. Numbed, I didn't answer.

My brothers had asked me to sing at Mama's funeral. I chose a song written by Andrae Crouch:

Through it all, through it all,
I learned to trust in Jesus,
I learned to trust in God.

As I sang those words, I meant them. I did learn to trust God through all the problems and difficulties as I was growing up. But I put off grieving because I had a problem within myself. Without realizing it, I had trained myself over the years to keep from dealing with pain.

Four months after Mama's death, Daddy died suddenly. Again I did not grieve. I had spent too many years smiling on the outside and crying on the inside. I didn't realize it, but these years were coming to an end.

Part Two

7

The Year of the Curse

"Blessed are those who mourn, for they will be comforted" (Matthew 5:4).

"Mary, you'll be up and at it soon. You'll be your old self again in no time," my missionary friend Peggy reassured me.

What does she know about it? I grumbled to myself. Then I cringed. *What has happened to me? She's right—I am discouraged. I'm not my once eager and happy self, ready to get on with the job.*

I looked around. The blue curtains stirred in the breeze blowing off East Africa's Lake Victoria. I wanted to sit right here in my quiet, cool, blue bedroom and forget about saving Africa's lost. Ever since coming back from furlough in America—the furlough immediately following Mama's death—my mind and body had seemed to be changing, and I was only thirty-four.

Without coming right out and saying it, people I had known and worked with tried to tell me that I was depressed. Others hinted I was nearing that "dangerous stage" in my life. Not knowing it then, my angry reaction to people came from a subconscious fear, the fear of an emotional breakdown at age thirty-nine—just like Mama. For the first time in my life I could not rise above my circumstances on my own.

My usual happy way of handling my work and my relationships was fast being replaced with a negative attitude. The more anger I felt, the more I suppressed it. This created more depression, and I was not able to admit my feelings because that would mean I would have to admit fear also. I was desperately afraid of reaching thirty-nine—it had become the year of the curse.

Delayed grief was slowly eating away at my mental stamina and steadily weakening my once determined disposition. I had changed and didn't know it.

First came the physical change. For a year I had regular bouts of malaria. Its fever weakened my body and I became susceptible to other diseases, such as amoebic dysentery. With these two illnesses and the strong medication required to rid my body of these parasites, I was losing ground.

Jimmy had tremendous strength and drive, even though he had had two major episodes of bleeding ulcers and surgery. I could no longer keep up with him, nor did I have the will to do so.

We had always scheduled our meetings together. He taught the men while I taught the women, and we did a lot of team teaching. But I was forced to stop much of this activity because of my illnesses.

Hundreds of women depended on me. "Mama Beggs, we miss you too much. You must come back; we have no one to teach us."

No good missionary would just walk out on these ladies. Neglecting my responsibilities caused me to feel guilty.

I had always been willing and ready to carry a part of the workload on the mission field, and my load had equaled many of the men's loads. But to keep up with Jimmy as I had done in the past was now quite impossible for me. Physical weakness brought a sinking of my spirit also. Jimmy had come a long way as a preacher since we met, and he didn't need me the way he used to. But I didn't know how to turn loose of the responsibility I had taken on when I had said, "You will be a good preacher, Jimmy. You'll see."

As laboratory tests revealed new cycles of both parasites in my blood and stool, I became even more discouraged. Furlough was three months away, but because of these diseases, Jimmy and I decided that I should go on to America immediately and get out of the tropics. Greg and Suzan could go with me and start the 1978–1979 school year in America instead of at the boarding school where they had attended most of their lives.

We reached Texas the beginning of August 1978. As I registered the kids, I looked at my petite and beautiful fourteen-year-old daughter. *Oh, God, keep her through this discouragement I'm experiencing,* I prayed. *But surely this feeling will pass. I'll get my strength back. By the time Jimmy gets here it will all be forgotten.*

"See you this afternoon, Mom," Greg said. Then he was gone. *He's already a junior,* I thought. Happy about having gotten my kids registered, I turned toward the car. It was the kids' first glimpse of American schools in over four years. I glanced in the direction Suzan had walked. It seemed like a long, long time ago since I was fourteen and in the ninth grade. That was the year my older sister had gotten married, and I had become a substitute mother.

I got in the car and went home to bed. From September through the end of November I stayed in bed most of the time. The recovery from constant amoeba and malaria was slow, but by Thanksgiving I began to feel stronger. Jimmy had come home, and I was encouraged.

But one day I received a phone call. "You were a rotten substitute mother and all of the younger kids do not respect you. You ruined our lives!" It was one of my sisters.

She's right, I thought. *I failed Mama and those little kids. I'm no good, and my life isn't worth living.*

78

It was true—I had not been a very good mother at age fourteen, or even by eighteen, but I had handled the situation like most fourteen-year-olds would have.

As long as I had had physical strength, I had been able to ignore my emotions, but when I started losing the energy to be on the go, my thoughts started catching up with me.

When my brothers and sisters talked about how they grieved for Mama and Daddy, I thought, *Why should I cry? Mama and Daddy are in heaven. Why should I go to the cemetery? They are not there—they are with Jesus.* I struggled to keep my feelings buried by trying to believe that I really didn't have them, but they were trying to surface more often now.

I felt unsettled in spirit with man and God. I needed desperately to win some battles in my thoughts. I was extremely tired spiritually, emotionally, and physically.

I have always believed environment has an effect on a person. I also believe that the person's will is the key to overcoming his environment. Hadn't I won over the environment when I was young, by graduating from high school, going to college, and becoming a missionary?

To win over the fear of this year of the curse, this fear that I was slowly admitting, I would have to bring my thoughts to Jesus. But the question in my mind remained: *Can I and will I fight or give up?* Mama had given up.

My intellect knew exactly what to do, but because I had been in a severe mental battle that was taking my strength, I wasn't able to assert my will as I once had.

The enemy was pressing hard. If I made my choice to fight with faith and win this battle, God's Spirit would support that choice and fight for me. *"For the Lord God, he it is that fighteth for you"—Joshua 23:10.* He would help me win through His Son Jesus.

I also believed if I chose not to fight, He would not cross my will.

It was certainly God's will for me to find peace in this situation. I allowed the phone call from my sister to sock me in the gut, but later I was thankful for it. It caused me to deal with some unfinished mental struggles and grief. My sister's words hurt, but they brought me to action.

Eventually I decided to take off the robe of guilt I had so easily slipped on—even though it would leave me emotionally naked. Closeted emotions were longing to be let out; grief for Mama and the little kids would unclothe me, expose me. But I had hidden for too long. Now I was ready to do what was necessary to start all over in my relationships.

Readjusting my thoughts toward Mama now that she was gone was simple and done quickly—compared to what it was like for Jimmy and me to make the needed changes in our relationship. Feelings toward Mama were in my past; Jimmy was in my present. One spouse can't go through a mental battle without it affecting the other. Being emotionally naked in front of Jimmy was difficult, for it would be my first time.

After my mama's death I kept my grief buried for five years. Two of those years I was physically sick. Near the end of my two-year bout of tropical illness, I knew I had come to the end of buried grief for Mama and my hurting relationship with Jimmy. Because they were intermingled I couldn't face one without facing the other.

Time for grieving has come, Mary! my subconscious demanded. And so I yielded to the demand. But if I had to be honest about Mama, I would have to be honest about Jimmy. *Dying would be easier*, I thought.

Many people I know do not agree with digging up the past. They say, "Pray about it and God will take care of it." God can't take care of our problems if we don't pray about them honestly. I had prayed all my life, but how could I be honest with God about things I hadn't been honest with myself about?

I didn't plan this year of the curse, but somewhere in my mind I had stored the fear of it. *I am like Mama.* "Junie, you are just like Mama." How many times she had told me this. I had been expecting to go into a deep depression at age thirty-nine just like Mama had done; 1978 was my year.

About the only thing I was really aware of during that year was the excruciating pain. Because of it I contemplated death rather than exposing my innermost feelings for Jimmy and Mama. I was paralyzed with fear.

When I recognized the weapons being used against me as fear and imaginations, I wanted to control them and not let them control me. For as long as my emotions were in the lead, I would lose for sure.

I had to find a way to regain my willpower with God's help. I had willed to give up, and I would will to regain that lost emotional strength. I had to allow the power of the Holy Spirit to again strengthen my will to choose.

I realized I had to find a way out of this muddle of fear, rejection, loneliness, and anger all mixed with imaginations—or I would destroy my marriage and my children's lives.

The torment slowly enshrouded my mind; plans of wanting to die began to form. Somewhere deep within me, though, was a stirring. "God, there has got to be another answer to this pain besides dying. Help me, God," I cried.

I couldn't work through this alone; I had to find someone to talk to. (I had not learned to lean on Jimmy about Mama's death.)

For two months I hadn't been able to sleep. I was reliving the past with Mama and the little kids and trying to redo what could not be redone. Fear was my pain and pain was my fear. "Oh, God, it hurts. I'm smothering under this debris in my life. Help me, God. Please help me. Show me what to do and how to do it."

Then the Holy Spirit began to help me realize what had been happening in my mental and emotional life, and what the hiding had done to me and the ones I loved. I knew all those years of masking my pain were coming home to me. I had to face them, walk through the pain again, and choose how to live with the consequences of those years of holding Mama above reproach and always hiding my true feelings.

Once I chose to face my past, God gave me strength. He was fighting for me.

Pushing myself to my elbows, I sat up and looked around my bedroom. I had never felt more alone, but I knew God was with me. "God, You and I are going to fix this," I prayed. "I have fixed many things before with Your help and I can fix this, too."

A determination rose up within me just like the determination I had had when I was four years old and had memorized the Christmas poem. I chose to curse the year that was trying to curse me: A battle had been won—the war was before me.

8

Looking for Answers

"So, remove vexation from your heart and put away pain from your body, because childhood and the prime of life are fleeting" (Ecclesiastes 11:10, NASB).

Nervously I dialed the number of a gynecologist recommended to me by a friend.

"Dr. Smith's office," a very business-like voice answered.

"When could I come for consultation and tests?" I asked, suppressing an impulse to let the whole story tumble out.

"We have had a cancellation," she said. "Would you like to come in this afternoon?"

God is at work already, I thought as I hung up the phone. He knew I was anxious and ready to take the first plunge in coping with my problems.

A few years earlier I had had a hysterectomy. Did this cause my mental struggle? I didn't know, but seeing the gynecologist for hormone level tests seemed like the first step I should take in determining my condition.

Later that afternoon I told the doctor, "Nothing works anymore. I have come to the dead end; I can't turn my mind off even long enough to sleep. I doze a couple of hours each morning, from five to seven. What is wrong with me?"

After a full examination the gynecologist said I was physically well: There were no signs of the malaria or amoeba in my system; my hormone level was normal. He recommended that I see a counselor he knew.

Now I had to acknowledge that I faced a mental battle, not a physical one. My physical systems may have registered normal, but my objectivity of spirit and mind was below zero.

Accompanying my fear were imaginations. My thought processes would not permit any logical way out of my depression. Fear and imaginations carried me far from the truth God longed for me to have. But I knew He wanted me to have the truth in my innermost being. "When He, the Spirit of truth, comes, He will guide you into all the truth" (John 16:13, NASB). Again, as when I was a little girl coming to Jesus, my choices in everyday living affected my being kept by the Holy Spirit's power—but this time it was on the battlefield of my mind.

What kind of fears bothered me? Some of the ones I was more conscious of concerned my own family. I felt unworthy to be the mother of my two precious children. The rejection I was battling I now projected toward my teenagers: If I had failed Mama's little kids, wouldn't I fail mine? Did they really need me anymore? Could I ever contribute to their lives again? Should I disappear? Wouldn't they be better off without me?

Lies! Lies from "the father of lies" (John 8:44, NASB). And convincing? Yes, very convincing. I thought Jimmy didn't need me anymore. *He doesn't express himself; he's closed to me*, I told myself. *I don't really know him because he won't let me in. Why does he shut me out? It would be better for all of us if I just ran away. Mama ran away, didn't she?*

"Stop it. Stop it!" I cried out. *I must not think these things.* I saw myself as a small boat lost at sea, rocked and slapped about by the waves of life, without a shore in sight. *And do you think anyone cares for you or knows about your pain?* I asked myself. *Of course not,* I responded. *You're like Mama, you know.* Disillusionment, anger at the past, guilt, terror of the future—it all tormented me.

The subconscious fear began surfacing—what was my identity with Mama? How much was I like her? I now entered an endless maze, my greatest fear yet. I didn't know why Mama had had a nervous breakdown at thirty-nine. I was in my thirty-ninth year, nearly forty. Mama had experienced that serious misunderstanding with the church she loved so—was that the reason for her breakdown?

The counselor and I went round and round on

this topic. He presented a theory of why Mama collapsed emotionally, but couldn't prove it.

Whatever Mama's reason had been, I still had to decide whether I would continue for years feeling fearful or would go on regardless of why Mama collapsed. Would I end up like Mama or not?

The counselor told me, "If your mother did lose her mind according to my theory, I want you to know I would never let that happen to you, Mary. I won't let you lose your mind."

I thanked him for caring for me that much and left the session feeling relieved. But only for a short while. I was more in bondage than ever. For the counselor had implied my future was up to him, and I followed the implication. I began to look to him as the one who would keep me from becoming like Mama. (I didn't realize that the choice was not up to him.) I clung to him through phone calls and appointments.

Even though I knew the Bible said that God was with me, my emotions ruled me, and I still felt alone. *I don't know why Mama lost touch with reality, so I can never bring my mind under control again*, I thought.

All the time the battle was raging, I was calling out to Jesus for help. I was reading God's Word and searching my past with the counselor. Some counselors are good, some better, and some poor. This one took too much control over me, and I suffered for it. I allowed him to take this control and reviled him for it later.

When Jesus was tempted, He said to Satan, "It is written: 'Worship the Lord your God, and serve him only'" (Matthew 4:10, NASB). I became so dependent on this counselor that I know I grieved the Spirit of God.

I felt the counselor would keep me from losing my mind. I gave him authority and control over my life. I can hardly believe how naive I was and how arrogant he was. I didn't realize it at the time, but I fell into a kind of worship of the man.

Later, I (this time with Jimmy) would go to another counselor who would be qualified both spiritually and professionally. We learned from him as he talked with us about our problems and helped us search for answers in God's Word. But the conclusion was that I had to choose for myself whether I wanted to come out of the depression or not. No one else had the key. If I lost my mind and couldn't function in reality, or if I sought and accepted ways to escape unreality, it would be because I had decided.

When this truth lit up my mind, I had much more mental and spiritual strength for the battle. Then I could progress.

I had chosen to go on in life and not let the dead hand of the past and my emotions about the past defeat me. What was I to do about my relationship with Jimmy? I was appalled at the garbage that appeared when I started being open in front of Jimmy. It lay between us deep, heavy, hot, and stinking.

But sometimes a relationship is like a damaged building. To be repaired, it must be taken down to the foundation and rebuilt—assuming the foundation is good. I loved Jimmy. I was committed to him with a vow before God—"until death do us part." I loved our God who had brought us together. Yes, the foundation was good! Brick by brick we would begin to rebuild.

9

Hold Me

"God is faithful; he will not let you be tempted beyond what you can bear. But when you are tempted, he will also provide a way out so that you can stand up under it" (1 Corinthians 10:13, NIV).

What would it be like to have married someone else? What would it be like to have someone hold me who really understands how I feel deep down inside? If I could find someone who could hold me until this pain goes away, I would rest there forever.

I would catch myself thinking those thoughts during that critical furlough year. Then the argument would begin in my mind: *What is wrong with me? I have Jimmy; he can hold me. . . . But when he does hold me, we don't seem to be aware of each other as people. God help me.*

Then came the humiliating shock of realizing I was attracted to my chiropractor. He was only adjusting my spine, but I actually wanted to ask him to hold me, to make the pain in my emotions go away just as he had made the pain in my back and neck go away.

How many times I had heard Christian women say, "I just do not understand how a woman can cheat on her husband. How can a woman, especially a Christian, come to the place that she can get involved with someone besides her husband?"

I used to have the same attitude. *How is it possible?* I wondered when tales were told of this one and that one who had fallen. Now I was beginning to understand how it happened.

"God, forgive me. This is not right. I know better, but I feel like I will die if I do not find someone stronger and bigger than me who will hold me until the storm has passed."

I began to feel extremely guilty. The more guilt I felt, the more I withdrew from Jimmy. Just the reaction the enemy wanted. If he could keep Jimmy and me estranged emotionally, perhaps he could destroy our relationship.

"To have and to hold, to love and to cherish. . . ." I had vowed before God to love and cherish Jimmy. And if our marriage was holy, as God had ordained it to be, then I was the only woman on earth whom Jimmy could hold in his arms with a love only we two shared. No other woman had this privilege. And Jimmy was the only man on earth who was to physically respond with the firmness and strength that a man's love brings. I was awestruck by this truth.

I had never really thought about our marriage being holy. I had simply assumed that that was because I married believing it was for life, "till death us do part." I took the sacredness of it for granted.

My honor and respect for Jimmy from the beginning of our married life had come easily enough. Our children knew we loved each other, and taking care of Jimmy and the children had come naturally for me. I prepared the meals, sewed on buttons, did the wash, and enjoyed it all.

But in my thirty-ninth year something began happening in my thoughts. I grew more and more angry at Jimmy because he had shut me out for so many years. This anger brought problems I never imagined I would encounter. Never before had I experienced the temptation of being attracted to another man. Jimmy was the only one for me.

I think I understand now how people fall into sexual sin. It all begins in one's thought life. This is difficult to talk about, but I feel I must bare my soul about this.

My desire to have a strong male hold me was so great that I wasn't able to look objectively at my thoughts. I was haunted with the idea that I must be wanting to have an affair. I could only conclude that I was turning out to be a very bad woman.

But sex was not my need, though I did not realize it at the time, and I was nowhere near being able to identify what my need was. And the longer I held these feelings inside of me, the stronger they became. I began to believe I would fall, and the more I believed it, the more I started putting it into action.

When I visited the chiropractor's office, I always made sure I looked especially nice. If he noticed me it would make me feel better about myself. *God knows I need to feel better about myself,* I rationalized. *Anyway, Jimmy is gone most of the time and doesn't see me. Come to think of it, I do not remember a time he ever told me I looked pretty. He compliments only that ministry stuff we no longer share. Ministry, ministry! Why can't I mean something to him as a person?*

I longed to be held by the counselor who had promised to not let me lose my mind. Surely, if he could hold me the pain would go away. Guilt followed these thoughts. This counselor was like my pastor—was I wanting my pastor to hold me! Surely I must be evil, lost, and forgotten by God.

"God, I didn't mean to turn out bad, but since I have, can You forgive me? Will You still love me?"

I was afraid of what people would do if they really knew me for what I had become. I wasn't the little, innocent girl-preacher most people from my past thought I was, I told myself. Instead, I had grown up to be a bad woman. *If they really knew me for who I am, they would turn their backs on me and wouldn't speak to me.*

I felt I should leave Jimmy and my children. *If they knew what I was really like now, they would want me to go,* I told myself over and over. *Besides, they don't really need me anymore. Jimmy is so closed to me, he wouldn't really care.*

When I felt I couldn't handle the inner struggle any longer, I decided to reveal my real self to Jimmy. I realized if I were to get help, he would have to come to my rescue. I couldn't fight the harassments anymore. Like a dry leaf at the will of the wind, I would eventually be crushed underfoot—unless my husband met me in this pain. Little by little I began to tell him what I was feeling.

Was I scared? I was petrified. I expected him to turn me out. Instead, he listened.

"For words like these to come from you, Mary," he said, "I know something is terribly wrong. You need my help. I never realized, never dreamed, you were being tormented like this and pushed to temptation. But I know this is not your usual way of life, Mary."

Jimmy forgave me. He understood, he cared, and he was trying to help me.

I saw grace at work in our marriage when Jimmy said, "This is my fault, too. We will work through this together."

Thank God I was forgiven by Jimmy. But I had to ask God's forgiveness, too. I had been the one who allowed these thoughts to take root. The suggestions had come from the enemy, yes, but I didn't expel them. I hadn't blocked them out with God's Word like I should have. I was the one who had committed emotional adultery. I had to repent and ask God to draw my mind back to Him and His Word.

When Jimmy said, "I know you want to win this battle in your mind, Mary, or you would not have told me about these temptations," the war was on its way to being won. The forgiveness I received from both Jimmy and God kept me on the right track. But I kept crying out to God for help. He knew my heart, and He miraculously intervened for me.

During this time of temptation I experienced pain between my shoulders, and I made an appointment to see a specialist. The night before my check-up, I dreamed about being in the doctor's office. I saw a man with reddish-colored hair and a mustache. I did not recognize him, but he was attending to me. As he bent over me, I heard a voice say: "Be careful. Be careful. Be careful."

The next morning at the doctor's office, I was told that another doctor was taking the place of my regular doctor for the day. When he came into the room, I gasped. This was the man I had seen in my dream. At first I wanted to excuse myself and leave, but then I thought, *No, God warned me for a reason, so this will be all right.*

In the course of our conversation, I realized

this man was hurting in his marriage as I was in mine. When he saw on my record that I was a missionary, he began to confide in me. I remained very quiet while he talked; I told him nothing about the problems in my own marriage or of the emotional estrangement between Jimmy and me. I left quickly.

I had understood the warning in the dream. Had God not cautioned me, I might have "naturally" entered into this man's emotional problem. I, in turn, could have shared mine. Emotionally we would have been reaching out to each other. But having been put on the alert by God, I had recognized my way of escape—to keep quiet.

I was glad that I had already started talking to Jimmy about my problem. Had we not already made a commitment to work on it together, I am not sure how this visit to the doctor might have turned out. I could have easily told my problems to the wrong person.

10
Taking Off the Smiles

"Laying aside falsehood, speak truth, each one of you, with his neighbor, for we are members of one another" (Ephesians 4:25, NASB).

Not communicating with Jimmy was almost worse than death. Over the years we had spent lonely nights lying side by side, for we were miles apart in spirit. I didn't know where I stood with him in his love for me.

Over the years, as Jimmy's ministry shifted into the area of administration, we talked less and less. The kind of ministry that had drawn us together was being left behind. And since Jimmy had never been expressive about our personal relationship, I was now getting no verbal feedback from him.

Jimmy's administrative duties brought him into close work with a colleague who I felt rejected me—both as a woman and as a minister. I tried at times in a light manner to tell Jimmy about this rejection, but he would only show more loyalty to the other person.

On one occasion I had worked long hours for many days helping Jimmy plan a conference. This type of work created a bond. During one of the sessions, the colleague singled me out and publicly said, "You cannot participate or vote here, because you are a woman."

I was stunned. I had known that the women probably wouldn't be allowed to vote; I hadn't come for that purpose. I was there to be a part of what Jimmy and I had created together. I needed to feel a part of what I had helped bring into being; this was a part of my identity, a part of the oneness I shared with my husband. But this person refused to respect our closeness on this project, as well as others over the years.

Jimmy was not present that day. I put on a smile and walked out of the session, pretending it didn't hurt. I thought, *It's okay. I'll be all right. This pain will pass and I can make it—I always have.*

Not telling Jimmy made it harder to bear the hurt, but because I didn't know what emotion I was fighting, I buried the incident. Our relationship suffered because I didn't face that pain until my thirty-ninth year. The pain I felt that day was like the pain I had felt as a little girl standing at the church door and being told, "You can't come in here." I felt again the nausea and the feeling of the grass pricking my legs as I sat down to cry—only this time the tears were frozen inside. I couldn't cry, not even in prayer to Jesus.

Because Jimmy had given his loyalty to his colleague instead of me, I eventually turned these negative emotions toward him and our marriage. Oh, how wrong it was! I had to learn to do as Ephesians 4:25,26 teaches us: "Laying aside falsehood, speak truth, each one of you, with his neighbor" (NASB).

But at the time, I buried the pain. And it turned to anger, then to disgust, and finally to disrespect for the person who had inflicted it. Many years later, after unearthing the pain, I would have to ask the fellow minister to forgive me.

Jimmy, too, had kept areas of his personal life hidden for years. "I know how to be truthful with facts," he said. "But I do not know how to be truthful with my deepest emotions."

Jimmy had been reared in an atmosphere where feelings were not openly expressed. He said, "Many times I sensed, 'You don't say things like that here; only positive feelings are acceptable.'" So frustration, anger, envy, and the like were stifled. It was a subtle form of dishonesty, but if we were to understand each other, it had to be dealt with.

The pain and sadness from not communicating took its toll on us: Often we couldn't sleep. When this began to happen, we realized we would have to take our marriage apart, fix the hurting areas, and put it back together, if our relationship was to survive.

During our 1978–1979 furlough, I had worked

through my pain over Mama and Daddy's deaths and how I raised my younger brothers and sisters. But Jimmy and I had barely begun on our needs as husband and wife. Slowly, however, as situations and circumstances presented themselves, we worked at our relationship.

One night at the dinner table we started talking. The African darkness and its sounds settled over us, but we hardly noticed. We finished the meal and moved to the couch, continuing to talk, searching for answers. We longed to know and understand each other better. We talked on until gray streaks of dawn touched the sky, for in those hours we started to genuinely express ourselves.

Crying, I said to Jimmy, "Perhaps this isn't real, this pain. Maybe we will wake up in the morning and it will all be a bad dream."

"No, I'm afraid it's very real," Jimmy answered.

I heard tears in his voice as he half prayed and half talked, "God, help us, and lead us to someone who can show us the way in this stage of our lives and thinking."

We talked about our differences and thoughts, discussed personality traits and needs. We searched for ways to know each other better, ways to close the distance between us created by pretended pleasantness.

We weren't thinking of ourselves alone. We reached out to our children, too. This was the year Greg was to leave Africa for college in the

United States. I dreaded his going ten thousand miles to live. Fighting guilt about Mama's kids, I was afraid I hadn't built into my son the stamina it took to be both African and American.

"What if he's not ready to go?" I wept to Jimmy. "Will he be open to the one he loves?" We tried to be careful about letting the children know exactly what was going on, but they knew we were suffering. Naturally, they suffered with us.

Later, the children told us, "We knew you loved each other and that seemed most important."

Slowly, over the next two years, God helped us to unmask, to take off the fake smiles and show each other where we were hurting. We learned things about each other that helped us know how we had arrived where we were in our relationship.

A program called Marriage Encounter opened our eyes to some of the corners we had never cleaned out in our relationship. We learned that feelings are neither right nor wrong; they just are. We compared this statement with what the Bible says. Jesus had a great range of feelings—anger, disappointment, pain, joy, peace, and loneliness. He was tempted in every way that we are, but did not sin.

When Jimmy realized this about Jesus, it freed him to admit his feelings. Feelings can be acceptable; it's how one reacts to them that can cause problems. For Jimmy to admit his feelings was to accept responsibility for them. He had to learn to be master of them, to make them his servants.

In learning to open up, Jimmy admitted he had always felt awkward and self-conscious in a group. When he was in high school, he would play hooky on oral report days, then make up the bad grades in some other way than an oral presentation. He was overwhelmed with feelings of inferiority. As a teenager his front teeth were badly stained and very crooked, which made him want to hide. Even though he had them fixed later, the damage to his confidence had been done.

Because of these early habits of hiding, Jimmy could not communicate with me now about his deep inner feelings. The only area he felt free to share with me was ministry. But by our mid-years, sharing the ministry was not enough for me. I needed words of approval to reassure me that our relationship had not gone stagnant.

We slowly continued taking apart and examining our relationship, and it hurt. It hurt like the night my mother had run away. The pain may have been a different kind, but it hurt nevertheless.

In our groping and searching I discovered something new and alive coming from Jimmy. He began to share himself with an openness we both needed. There is a great difference between just talking about things and being open with each other. Jimmy began to take a long look inside himself. He felt as exposed as the time he had been swimming in a lake and someone had hid his clothes. He had had to sneak home.

Jimmy's mask had been his buddy for a long time. He called it the mask of Mr. Anonymous: "Don't call attention to me, just let me hide in the group." But as he slowly began to talk about those hidden hurts, inferiority feelings, and characteristics he thought I might not like about him, he was taking off his mask and showing his pain to me. I cried when I learned some things about my husband he had hidden for years.

I remembered the time he had been ill with bleeding ulcers and had to have surgery. Unspoken and untouched feelings had been buried so deep he could not identify his true emotions. As a result, he seemed to have no feelings, to be unconcerned about his condition, and distant. I had actually thought, *If I walk out of his life, he will not care.*

I would say, "What is the matter with you, Jimmy? Have I done something?"

"Nothing," he would reply, knowing I didn't believe it.

I felt I was talking into a dead mike—I received no emotional feedback to monitor the relationship.

Later, as we examined our relationship, Jimmy said, "I hurt as I look at our marriage. I heard you but I didn't hear you; I saw you but I didn't see you. You said to me in a hundred and ten ways, 'Jimmy, I need you to compliment me, to talk to me, to hold me.' I remember times you changed something in the house, wore something different, got a new hairdo, and yet because of my own feelings of inferiority and self-doubt I could not see your needs. I could not give the approval you needed. Now I realize I need to acknowledge your presence by listening, hearing, and touching you."

Silence had overlaid the feelings in our relationship like so much tarnish on a neglected loving cup. Through the years the tarnish builds up . . . never getting polished away . . . until any inscriptions of devotion are blurred, unreadable.

Breaking the silence, expressing our true feelings, we began to experience an excitement, a newness, in our relationship. As we defied the estrangement, dropping the various masks we wore, we found ourselves getting reacquainted.

Learning to know Jimmy was a revelation to me. I realized that many times in our marriage I had had no grasp of his point of view. I was hiding my feelings to protect him and myself. He was hiding his to protect himself. No wonder we didn't communicate.

And had we not begun to share, my own struggle would have destroyed us.

11

Ministry Vs. Marriage?

by Jimmy Beggs

"'Take heed to the ministry which you have received in the Lord, that you may fulfill it'" *(Colossians 4:17, NASB).*

Ministry first or family? This is a common debate among people involved in people-helper ministries. But if one allows the family to disintegrate because of not caring for their physical and emotional needs, he will have no base to work from in helping others.

The Bible says that the bishop, or minister, must live the Word of God before being qualified to minister. (See 1 Timothy 3:1–7; Titus 1:5–9.) Therefore, proper relationships come before ministry; in fact, these relationships are prerequisites to ministry. When a minister says, "My ministry comes first," what does he mean?

We tend to divide the events of life into two categories: the sacred and the secular. We have sacred and secular days, sacred and secular places, sacred and secular clothes.

Not surprisingly, when we seek "a place for everything and everything in its place," we don't always find it—or we put that item where it doesn't belong. For example, all the parts of marriage and family do not seem to find their way into the sacred category.

But why do we go to all that trouble? God doesn't make these distinctions, we do. The question of sacred or secular, ministry or marriage, doesn't need to be asked.

All the events of our marriage—sex in the bedroom, chatting in the living room, cooking in the kitchen, and cleaning in the laundry room—should be lived out as a spiritual union. They are the sacred threads that make up the spiritual robe of marriage.

Paul listed spiritual qualifications for deacons and pastors in the Book of Timothy. Most of these qualifications have to do with the everyday events of life, such as maintaining self-control, offering hospitality, managing money, training our children to be obedient, and taking time for our family. And in the heart of this writing, Paul states, "If a man does not know how to manage his own household, how will he take care of the church of God?" (1 Timothy 3:5, NASB). True spiritual leadership is intricately related to how we live our lives with our spouses and families.

My wife and I were a close team once. We were yoked together with a common call and bond. Our ministry together brought us happiness, and we had the same attitudes, philosophy, and emotions toward this common bond.

Then I began to pull away from that bond, getting more and more involved in administrative responsibilities and positions. I was quickly leaving our combined ministry and spending hours and weeks planning for events and functions that did not involve Mary. Our conversations with each other became superficial.

I developed new loyalties. My loyalty to my wife and the home was conflicting with my loyalties to national pastors, the work program, and other individuals. I felt the pressure of being separated from my family. I, too, felt alone. My wife and I were living together, and yet we were far apart. Then I realized I needed Mary, that I had needed her all along. Realizing that our need for each other still existed, we searched for another common bond to replace the former one of ministry.

When Mary and I began to examine our marriage relationship, I was reminded of when I was a boy and a job of mine was to clean and maintain the cisterns. In the springtime, rainwater was funneled into the open cistern; in the winter we shoveled snow into the cistern to make fresh water. We used the water for home consumption.

Periodically, these cisterns accumulated debris that had to be cleaned out so the water could still be used. Part of my job as a boy was to help keep the cistern clean. I was let down by a rope through the narrow opening at the top of the well to where the cistern got wider and the water deeper. I had to look for cracks in the brick wall. Sometimes frogs or snakes or trash had to be removed from these cracks.

As the water got lower during the summer, we checked again for cracks. They had to be repaired so the water wouldn't leak out.

I feel Mary and I have had a good marriage because our foundation was good, even before we began to examine the relationship and do some cleaning out. We had personal times together for years. We prayed together, had family devotions, and took long walks on a regular basis. We had been developing good habits.

The typical distractions of life, such as television, school schedules, and family matters, were never a burden for us. But not all distractions are external. The debris in our marriage was caused by our simply ignoring areas we should have regularly tended.

My greatest distraction was internal: a lifelong fear of being open, transparent, about my deep feelings. I still catch myself wanting to throw a blanket over such emotions, to pretend they aren't there. I'm more comfortable that way. But it's a temptation to be squelched. And I'm grateful our togetherness does that.

Our togetherness is like the cistern full of pure, fresh water supplied by the rains. For years our home was centered around God and the ministry, and we did our best with each other and the children. Yet our marriage, like the cistern, collected some debris, developed some cracks.

Examining our marriage was like going down into the cistern. We identified some debris to remove, attitudes to work on. We became more aware of unseen, unspoken needs. We also saw that many good bricks were still in place.

The cleaning out has been good—painful, but good. I would do it all again to have what we have now.

12

Learning To Lean

"A time to mend" (Ecclesiastes 3:7).

One of the first steps to building a better, stronger marriage was our willingness to be open in sharing with and listening to each other. First, we examined our personalities and our intimate relationship, which were affecting our marriage. Then we started building a new union of our personalities and a new intimacy within our marriage.

In Genesis 2:24 God says, "They shall be one flesh," speaking of a husband and wife's intimate relationship. Jimmy and I are one flesh; yet at the same time we have two separate bodies, each with a separate set of thought patterns. Our thoughts are created from the experiences each of us has had from birth to the present.

I could cling to Jimmy and be one flesh in physical intercourse, but to get into his mind and know his pattern of thinking was not that simple—especially when we had a communication problem from the beginning. Jimmy's constant withdrawal, his inability to say, "I need you, Mary," made it difficult for me to open up to him or to listen to him.

At this point, too, our needs had influenced our children's lives, for Jimmy saw in our daughter some of our inabilities to share thoughts and needs. But she made a most providential decision. Although Greg would be leaving, Suzan would be remaining at home to study for her junior and senior years (instead of returning to boarding school).

Thus a very beautiful thing took place during our "home schooling" year of 1981–1982. We had come across John Powell's book *Why I'm Afraid To Tell You Who I Am*. For months, each morning in devotions we studied this book together. I saw a miracle take place as we all three worked on being open. Suzan unfolded like a flower before us. She looks back on that year as one of her best memories of home.

We all grew through those times of sharing and learning about ourselves. Understanding Jimmy just by listening to his words had been frustrating, because he couldn't tell me his feelings—negative or positive.

Then it dawned on me that over the years I had achieved some understanding of my husband by listening to what he was not saying. And that was a starting point. I began giving even more time to listening to what he was not saying, and I discovered a lot of pain.

The closer I listened, the more I learned about this man I loved but knew little about. I had always felt overpowered by Jimmy's physical and mental strength, but I was learning that he had a little boy in him who needed to be let out. I now felt for the first time like I was hearing the message from Jimmy's heart, not just the words from his mouth.

But openness is both giving to and receiving from each other. Until we began examining our relationship I couldn't confront Jimmy with any negative feelings about him. But as we really looked at ourselves we developed a beautiful understanding and joy we had never known with each other.

For example, Jimmy took me to a banquet attended by many people he knew but I did not. We had just come home from Africa, and I was feeling lonely and unsure of myself in a new city and unfamiliar setting. Jimmy started introducing me to others: "Walter, meet Mary, my wife. Marge, I'd like you to meet Mary."

Then suddenly someone diverted Jimmy's attention, and he left me for a while. As I stood there smiling and making myself known to his colleagues, I thought, *When we get home, I'll remind Jimmy not to leave me standing alone like this again.*

In the past, I wouldn't have admitted something like that—much less acted on it. But now I was free to express my true feelings to Jimmy. He listened, and it helped us both.

Yes, in working our way back to each other we got discouraged, but we didn't quit. We worked constantly at being open with our feelings.

Once when we were discussing another topic we disagreed on, Jimmy said, "This makes me angry. I feel really angry."

I ran over to him and touched his face. "You said you were angry. That's wonderful." We both started laughing. We knew we were growing.

Just as it was an adjustment for Jimmy to share with me, it was an adjustment for me to deliberately listen to his feelings. I feared cutting him off before he got through expressing himself. I feared trying to take it from him before he finished telling me his pain or joy.

I remember one night we were in bed, discussing something we had always looked at differently. I got discouraged with myself in trying to understand him.

"Oh, good grief, Jimmy! Why do we have to be so different?" Luckily, that question didn't end our communication. Instead, he got inspired, pointing out the advantages of our being different, and we both held each other, with him laughing and me crying.

I am not mechanical. I never have been. But Jimmy is extremely talented in that area. He used to say, "Mary, just turn the handle and lift the screw at the same time, and it will work. It's easy, can't you see that?"

I would cringe and feel hurt. I thought he was talking down to me. But now I don't allow it to hurt. I simply say, "No, I cannot see that, and

I can't make it work. I am not mechanical, can't you see that?"

The pressure is off, and we can both laugh or at least agree, and then we can do something with that gadget my mind does not understand.

Jimmy and I are different, and we always will be, but our differences or topics of disagreement can be blended in tenderness and caring enough to speak the truth in love (see Ephesians 4:15).

Once during our period of putting our marriage relationship back together, I heard Jimmy pray in our devotions, "God, give me new insight. Open my eyes to see all the good, the beautiful, and also that which I'm afraid of—that which might hurt and be hard to look at."

Afraid? Jimmy afraid? I was so surprised to hear him say he was afraid. His openness helped me to be willing to listen more to what fears a man might have. I knew these feelings were real, that he was hurting, and that it took courage for him to voice these fears to God in my presence. Remembering his shyness through the years then made me love him all the more.

By being open and listening to each other, we learned to exchange feelings. I often said, "Jimmy, sometimes all I need to know is that you heard me express my feelings. Then I can work through them." To exchange words and to exchange feelings are two completely different ways to communicate. We exchanged feelings in order to grow, to race against time and meet each other at the bottom of the stairs so we could climb back up together each time we hit a rough place.

A second step in our putting things back together was simple: We had to decide to love each other regardless of our communication problems. Marriage Encounter taught us that love is a decision. Through my floundering to find the closeness I had lost with Jimmy because of wearing masks, I was daily making a decision to love this man I had vowed before God to love and cherish. Although at times I felt we were separated emotionally (and I'm sure Jimmy felt this same spiritual estrangement), each step I took in trying to find my way back to him in spirit and togetherness was a decision to continue loving him.

Jimmy often said, "Love is not just how we feel at the moment; it's a commitment to a course of action."

A third step in putting it back together was learning to lean on each other in areas we had never before trusted each other. Especially during the year of the curse, I had to change my independent attitude or go under. Without Jimmy's compassion and his reaching out to me, I would have had a longer and more difficult time winning my mental battle.

For example, if I got too tired, my mind would run wild at night. One night after we had started being open and honest, I reached over to Jimmy and in tears asked him to pray that I could go to sleep. I felt emotionally harassed; fear kept me awake—I was going to end up like Mama!

In my mind I kept seeing her sitting and writing. I was struggling to get past this painful and fearful memory. As the pressure built inside of me, I kept thinking, *Oh, if I could call the counselor. He promised to never let me lose my mind.* But instead, as I half prayed and sorely fought for my sanity, I turned to Jimmy, and something happened. He then turned to me. He laid his hand quietly on me and asked God to help me. He kept his hand there and began talking.

"I need you, Mary. For the first time I realize I need to tell you how much you mean to me. Fight—for your sake first. Then fight for the kids and me. We want you; we stand with you. Mary, you will be all right. You will come through this, you'll see."

That was the moment Jimmy and I switched roles. He became the confident and committed supporter. I meekly clung to his words and his prayer. I actually saw a tiny glimmer of hope— surely I wouldn't lose my mind after all.

As a result of leaning on Jimmy, I knew I was no longer alone. He calmed and comforted my restless and uneasy spirit. And when he built me up, I let him know what he had done for me. We built up each other; we leaned on each other. It was mutual; it was complementary.

Confidence in Jimmy returned to me as we struggled, cried, and tried. The trying and relying brought elation and hope for our relationship. In leaning on Jimmy, I was enabled to walk back into the warmth of God's love.

13

Weapons for the Fight

"The weapons we use in our fight are not the world's weapons, but God's powerful weapons, with which to destroy strongholds" (2 Corinthians 10:4, TEV).

Although on paper my struggle may seem simple and short-lived, in reality the fight was long and difficult. Along the way I discovered some weapons to use in the fight. I began to use these weapons against the enemies of fear and imaginations. I learned about most of the weapons from self-help studies and from God's Word.

First, as I explained in the last chapter, I had to learn to lean on Jimmy, bringing us closer to each other and creating a world in which we could lovingly share.

Second, I had to learn to recognize the beginning of a damaging thought pattern. I realized many of my thoughts did not, in fact, belong to me; they came from the master of darkness and deceit, Satan himself. When one negative thought would come, another followed. Philippians 4:8 became a strong defense for me—

"Whatsoever things are true, whatsoever things are honest, whatsoever things are just, whatsoever things are pure . . . think on these things." I asked God to clear my mind of any thought that did not measure up to this verse.

I refused to dwell on thoughts that depressed me. True, negative situations are a part of life, but once I monitored my thoughts and worked through any negative incidents that happened during a day, I then refused to think on them further. This took tremendous willpower. I reclaimed my power of choice by the Holy Spirit's help of discerning these things that affected me in a negative manner.

Some negative situations never can be solved. This too I accepted, and then refused to dwell on those problems. I remembered the verse from 1 Peter 5:7: "Casting all your care upon him; for he careth for you." I often stopped and said, "Jesus, I can't do this alone. Rescue me from this thought at this very moment. I will my mind to be subjected to You now in Your Name." This mental exercise became a powerful tool. I used it thousands of times—sometimes resting in the struggle and other times taking the peace by spiritual force.

Thoughts about matters I could not prove, thoughts about what only *might* happen, I rejected. My pain was lessened by "bringing into captivity every thought to the obedience of Christ" (2 Corinthians 10:5).

Third, I replaced negative thoughts with the Word. I paraphrased verses I had memorized that told me the opposite of the damaging thought. Doing this killed the thought before it could take root. If I couldn't quote the Scripture word for word, at least I got the essence of its meaning in my mind. For example, when I thought, *I may never know peace again*, I would tell myself, "Jesus said He came to give me peace. I choose His peace in His Name now" (see John 14:27).

I said these words out loud if I was alone. If the negative thought kept returning to me, I wrote down the positive one and said it to myself until the darkness lifted. Sometimes I would battle a thought for days. But slowly, I recovered spiritual ground that belonged to me as a child of God.

Another constant thought that plagued me was, *If God cared about you, you wouldn't have to struggle like this.* I would reply, "The God of peace says He will keep me if I think on Him. I will myself to trust Him; He is keeping me now" (see Isaiah 26:3).

As I took God's Word and applied it to my situation, I believed that through His power I was the victor.

I used God's Word in another way: My head knew and believed God's Word, but my emotions kept lying to me. My feelings were real, but I had to recognize them as feelings only—which did not always correspond to fact. Because I refused to give up and because in faith I read and recited God's Word consistently, I was one day able to choose what it says about His strength being in the believer rather than accept the emotions and feelings that ruled me.

When this happened, my mind became clear; the darkness lifted. There were times of regression, but again, I clung to God, and His Spirit fought for me.

I believed that I couldn't be free from pain until I had some understanding of the cause of the pain. If the cause was unresolved, then I would make a choice to accept that, as I had about the cause of Mama's emotional collapse. Making a choice gave me strength.

(Yes, one often hears, "Cast it off. Lay it aside. Give it up." These words are true, but if I spoke them as glibly as I sometimes heard them—before mentally working through the grief or pain—they only brought more confusion.)

Fourth, I prayed in the Spirit and the Spirit himself prayed for me when I did not know how to pray in my own language (Romans 8:26,27). Such praying helped; I knew I was talking to God according to 1 Corinthians 14:15 ("I will pray with the spirit"), and I felt safe praying this way.

Emotional healing is no different than physical healing. It can be instant or it can be gradual, as we walk by faith, day by day. I had hidden from myself, Jimmy, and the world for years,

and it took time, God, and determination to regain the truth I had lost in that hiding.

Fifth, I took physical action. I drove to the
cemetery where my parents had been buried.
Sitting down by their graves, I began talking
to them. Whatever thoughts surfaced I told
them, weeping as I did. I knew they couldn't
hear me, but it was a method of release for me.
I cried until I could cry no more. I cleaned out
each room of my life that I had shut the door
on as a child. I forgave Mama for dying before
I got home from Africa when I hadn't seen her
for four years.

But I found even more difficult the act of for-
giving Mama for sitting in her own world days
at a time while the little kids and I struggled
with daily living. I loved Mama very much and
that was part of the reason I held so much anger
toward her.

Phoning old friends, I asked lots of questions
about our family's past. For the first time I talked
openly with some of my older brothers and sisters about Mama's problems. Then I asked forgiveness from all the younger ones for failing
them. I never gave up.

Sixth, I repented of my anger, which had become a very subtle form of rebellion. This alone
had been enough to give the enemy a foothold
in my life.

Seventh, I avoided smug people with self-
righteous and clichéd answers for depression. I
remember thinking, *I will accept your clichés*

and pat answers if you will tell me how to apply them to this excruciating pain.

How does God judge a person who, when the pain, burden, or responsibility, gets too heavy, retreats or avoids reality? Who can really answer such a question? I can't. But I do know that turning emotional pain over to Jesus when the enemy had a grip on my mind was hard mental work. Yet as long as I was trying, the Holy Spirit didn't give up on me. I had to strive to reach peace and safety, but freedom of mind became "life and truth" when I received it by walking out of darkness into Jesus' light. (See John 3:20,21; 8:12; and 14:6.)

Through chaos and pain, Jesus kept my marriage. It could have been lost forever, for my husband and I were emotionally estranged in our middle years. But we made the choice to fight for what had already been given to us: a marriage sealed in heaven to be kept by our Lord and Savior—even in severe temptation! I know God's Word. With every temptation He will make a way to escape . . . but we must choose it.

Epilogue

Many times when I look at my husband I feel a surge of gratitude to God. Our Father in heaven was so faithful to keep us when we needed Him! I believe our honesty with ourselves and God brought us through the period I have just described.

As I write this epilogue I can feel the cool breeze of the beginning rains in Nairobi, Kenya. Tonight, I am alone. Jimmy, along with our regional leader, has gone to Malawi, Africa. He went there to represent East African School of Theology in a meeting, for he is its interim president.

Jimmy's first interest though is International Christian Center, also located here in Nairobi. He loves pastoring this unusual church. Presently the congregation averages over two hundred and is growing. It is rewarding to lead Muslims and Hindus to Jesus. Watching them grow in the Word and in their Christian walk is just as exciting. We are in the process of looking for another building. We have outgrown the present one.

And where do I fit into this picture? Right by Jimmy's side. I carry a heavy visitation schedule since he is doing two major jobs right now. I go into homes and have Bible studies three and four days a week. One of these homes is that of a former Catholic who, due to ill health, is unable to attend church; another home belongs to a former Muslim, who is crippled. Both have been saved. A third person is a Hindu, also crippled. He is keenly interested in becoming a Christian. Others are new converts interested in the Word.

In a church where Indians, Africans, and Caucasians all have different needs, a pastor's wife has many other duties as well.

Of course, the correspondence and bookwork of a missionary are never caught up. The days are full and happy ones as we grow older together in life and in Jesus.

Greg finished Central Bible College in 1984. He chose a wonderful girl named Danna Whitney, also a C.B.C. graduate, as his wife. They just completed two years of pastoral work in West Texas. Not long afterwards they received their appointment as Assemblies of God missionaries to Tanzania (for they have both felt the call to missions work). This is the country we first lived in when we came to Africa in 1964. The little boy who threw rocks into the dark while waiting for a ride from the airport so many years ago is still as full of energy as then.

How grateful we are that his energy will be

spent in following his daddy's footsteps into missions! Greg and Danna, however, have a vision quite different from any Jimmy and I have ever known. They hope to lead Muslim people to Jesus. We feel they will make an excellent team.

Being from Texas, they say it's okay to be proud. Well, we do give thanks to God for them both. They have blessed our lives and are a source of encouragement to us.

Presently, they are itinerating, raising funds to be in Africa sometime in early 1988. They will meet that goal at the rate they are going. Greg's ministry ability helps him in this responsibility.

Our daughter, Suzan, received her A.A. degree in 1984 from Central Bible College also. Not long afterwards she married an Evangel College graduate, Timothy Loren Triplett of Springfield, Missouri. We finished that wedding and all its trimmings one week and headed for Africa the next. It was emotional, but what a joy and peace we felt about their union!

Tim and Suzan have copastored in Missouri, been senior pastors in Texas, and are youth pastors. They love the Lord and each other.

Suzan had surgery as a little three-year-old. Doctors told her that she would never be able to carry a baby because the surgery was in the bladder and kidney area. Her faith won! She had a beautiful little girl named Sarah in April 1986. Jimmy and I are now grandparents!

Home for Tim and Suzan is First Assembly of God in Lubbock, Texas. They work with Pastor Tom Lakey. I cannot describe to you the feelings of goodness and mercy having followed me when I share with you about both our children being in the ministry. We thank God for Tim and his love for our daughter, Suzan. God has been so, so good to us through our children.

Having a grandbaby is another era all its own. Surely these beautiful feelings come straight from the heart of God! We love that Sarah.

Many people write and say things like, "How do you stand it? Leaving that grandbaby in America and living so far away?" I guess I always answer by saying, "I don't dwell on it." Sure, it hurts—but my hope and confidence in our maturing marriage relationship makes all pain easier. We like us both better; we are together now in mind and spirit. That makes all the difference in my outlook on life.

Pain from the past does not seem to surface. Since that unfinished business of mourning was taken care of, I can look at it with a very healthy veiw: Mama and Daddy are gone; one cannot stop life. Neither have Jimmy and I returned to a counselor since examining and rebuilding our relationship; we work things out on our own. For besides no longer hiding anything from one another, every day we pray together and spend time in God's Word.

Jimmy and I now have dimensions of trust that we had never known in some areas. We share our weaknesses, fears, and temptations, along with our love and desire for each other. We have recaptured our first love. The renewed feeling of togetherness has infused us with vigor for facing the future—we anticipate more good years of choosing and loving.

Probably one of our greatest struggles today would be in having to slow down. Although I stay very busy, I pause more than I did when I was younger! Living in the tropics does not allow us to keep the pace we once did. And Nairobi is a pleasant place to live. But our health is simply not as good as it was before Jimmy's stomach surgery and my emotional battle. We gave the devil an opportunity when we refused to speak the truth in love (see Ephesians 4:25–27).

Yet, this struggle has its rewards! We know where our help comes from—"from the . . . Maker of heaven and earth" (Psalm 121:1,2, NIV). When we have put in a full day's work of preaching, praying, administrating, and so forth, we are aware that our help has been from God. We trust Him daily for our strength; that is a choice we make—just one more choice of the last few years I know the Lord has been pleased with!